Our Favourite Poems

Our Favourite Poems

New Zealanders choose their best-loved poems

INTRODUCTION BY IAIN SHARP

craig potton publishing

ACKNOWLEDGEMENTS

The publishers would like to thank Gwen Redshaw who first suggested publishing a New Zealand version of this concept; the *Sunday Star-Times* for their promotion of the voting process and for continuing to support New Zealand publishing through their book review pages; Iain Sharp for his heartfelt introduction; the New Zealand booksellers and libraries who promoted both the voting and the book; and all the many New Zealanders, both young and old, who voted for their favourite poem and made the whole exercise such a pleasure.

First published in 2007 by Craig Potton Publishing
98 Vickerman Street, PO Box 555, Nelson, New Zealand
www.craigpotton.co.nz

Compilation © Craig Potton Publishing
Poems © Individual copyright holders

Cover design: Oriel Design

ISBN 978-1-877333-68-2

Printed in New Zealand by PrintStop, Wellington.

CONTENTS

IAIN SHARP

INTRODUCTION

One afternoon in early spring, while I was thinking about what to say in this introduction, my friend Joy and I went to have lunch at a favourite spot, the tearoom in Eden Gardens on the lower slopes of Mount Eden. Omana Avenue, the approach road to the gardens, is lined with Taiwanese cherry trees, which were in full bloom. More tui than I had ever seen before in one place at one time, 40 or 50 of them, swooped deliriously from bough to bough, glutting themselves on the nectar of the luscious pink blossoms. Some had consumed so much they were puffed up to almost spherical dimensions. Parson birds, the early European settlers decorously called them, but they were behaving on this occasion more like bloated whisky priests.

Unbidden, lines I had learned nearly 40 years ago came to mind: 'Loveliest of trees, the cherry now/ Is hung with bloom along the bough.' It was my good luck to have an exceptional English teacher, Reg Lockstone, for three of my five high school years. I was in a science stream (maths, chemistry, physics), but very few of us went on to become scientists. Two of my former classmates now run language schools. Others are journalists. Reg's influence ran deep. Bringing to his subject an infectious passion, he communicated a delight in verbal resourcefulness that stayed with us long after memories of algebraic equations and experiments with beakers and Bunsen burners had dimmed. A poetry-lover, he could recite much verse by heart, including the poem by Alfred Edward Housman I have just quoted.

Housman, writing in the 1890s, had as his focus the white-flowering cherry found in his beloved Shropshire (*Prunus avium*, is it? I'm no botanist) rather than the candyfloss-coloured variety that the Omana Avenue tui were relishing and ravishing (*Prunus campanulata*, I discover from Google). Although Housman was famed for his erudition, the term 'Taiwanese cherry' would have perplexed him, for in his day the island of Taiwan was still known as Formosa. With no particular interest in New Zealand, he probably had little notion what a tui was either. The fit was thus hardly exact, but Housman's eloquent lines still seemed somehow apposite and I was pleased to recall them.

Plenty of New Zealanders must think likewise, for 'Loveliest of Trees' is embraced in this book as one of our favourite poems. When I flick through the anthology, however, it's not just the inclusion of Housman's lyric that reminds me of that spring afternoon with the tui feasting merrily on exotic foliage. A similarly relaxed intermingling of the indigenous and the imported can be found in these pages. Denis Glover, who famously disavowed any interest in 'quaint old England's quaint old towns', preferring to 'think of what will yet be seen in Johnsonville and Geraldine', is nevertheless discovered here rubbing shoulders with Rudyard Kipling and Alfred Noyes. Bill Manhire and Brian Turner shake hands with Hilaire Belloc and Gerard Manley Hopkins. Margaret Mahy slings an arm around Elizabeth Barrett Browning. Hone Tuwhare gives a hongi to Tennyson and Shakespeare.

In 1995, when the literary-minded British television programme *The Bookworm* asked viewers to name their all-time favourite poems, thousands responded to the poll. Votes were collated and the hundred most popular choices were published in an anthology titled, with pleasing simplicity, *The Nation's Favourite Poems*. The book was enough of a success for several sequels, arranged more thematically, to follow in its wake. Within a few years there were collections of Britain's favourite comic poems, love poems, animal poems, poems of childhood, poems of journeys, poems of desire and poems of celebration.

In July 2007 Craig Potton Publishing decided to try a similar survey in New Zealand. Few restrictions were placed on local voters. They were free to nominate from any country and any century. If they wanted to choose several offerings from the same author, that was fine too. The idea was promoted through bookshops, libraries, schools and the *Sunday Star-Times*. The response was so hearty that the original cut-off date had to be extended to include all the people who wanted to participate.

Comparing New Zealanders' favourite hundred poems with the equivalent British list has proved a fascinating process. As you might expect, the biggest difference relates to local content. The first British anthology contained two poems from Robert Frost ('Stopping By Woods on a Snowy Night' and 'The Road Not Taken') and one each from Henry Wadsworth Longfellow (an excerpt from 'Hiawatha') and Edgar Allan Poe ('The Raven'). Otherwise all the contributions came from within the British Isles, unless you want to be pedantic and insist on returning that quintessentially English banker T.S. Eliot to his Missouri origins and on calling Kipling an Indian because his parents happened to be in Bombay at the time of his birth. No Antipodean writers got the nod from British selectors.

New Zealand voters were more wide-ranging. As well as Poe, Frost and Longfellow (from whom we prefer the succinctness of 'The Slave's Dream' to the rather repetitive 'Hiawatha'), the American bards we invite into our homes include Maya Angelou, Billy Collins, E.E. Cummings, Emily Dickinson and Max Ehrmann (the Indiana attorney who wrote 'Desiderata'). If we're not especially generous to our Australian cousins, we do at least give the thumbs-up to a couple of 'Banjo' Paterson classics ('The Man from Snowy River' and 'The Man from Ironbark').

Most significantly, however, we happily endorse the home-grown product. Tuwhare's 'Rain' was the poem which received most votes overall and the runner-up was Glover's 'The Magpies'. 'Oh great,' I can hear curmudgeons mumble, 'our top pick is a poem about lousy weather, followed by a harsh saga of financial ruin and unpaid mortgages. That shows what a miserable bloody bunch we Kiwis are.'

I take the point, but I don't agree with it. 'Rain' is not in the least miserable. On the contrary, it's a marvellously sensuous cry of joy in everyday occurrences. (As an Aucklander, I'll concede to the curmudgeons that, yes, in my part of the world rain occurs almost every day.) The poem's speaker might have few material possessions, but he has a richness of the spirit that cannot be taken away from him. When Hone wrote 'Rain' in the late 1960s,

I think he was still working as a boilermaker – a very noisy occupation that no doubt contributed to the increasing deafness which plagues him today. Still, there's an innate musicality in the man that hearing problems will never extinguish. I feel confident that in selecting 'Rain' as our number one favourite we made the right choice. Kia ora, Hone.

There are conflicting theories about how Glover came to write 'The Magpies'. The one I like best identifies the poem's 'Tom and Elizabeth' as Glover's old friend and fellow bard Thomas Allen Curnow (who seldom used his first name) and Curnow's first wife, Betty (the subject of one of Rita Angus's finest portraits). Sometime in the 1940s, so the story goes, after working in the newspaper business for many years without developing a taste for it, Curnow spoke of chucking in journalism and taking up farming instead. 'The Magpies' was Glover's mocking retort. The emotional scope of the poem goes far beyond mockery, however. Those interminably chattering magpies might be indifferent to the plight of Tom and Elizabeth, but not Glover. Although he was a city boy, born in Dunedin, raised in New Plymouth, Auckland and Christchurch and later a long-time resident of Wellington, he always had a ready sympathy for the hard-scrabble lives of rural strugglers. Compassion for people down on their luck is one of the most attractive Kiwi attributes, I reckon. It amuses me, though, to think of bookish visitors from overseas who politely inquire what New Zealand's most famous lines of poetry might be – and are greeted with a raucous squawk: 'Quardle oodle ardle wardle doodle!'

Tuwhare and Glover both appear twice in the book. 'No Ordinary Sun' and 'Arawata Bill' are the other poems of theirs to make the cut. Hone was part of J Force, which had the task of supervising Japanese repatriation at the end of World War II. He visited Hiroshima and saw at first hand the destruction wrought by nuclear weapons. Glover never met gold prospector William O'Leary (the real-life 'Arawata Bill' – a hardy old buzzard if there ever was one), but he claimed in later life that as a boy he had once or twice glimpsed doughty Bill tramping along in the distance. He based his poem on tales supplied by a mountaineering friend, John Pascoe, who had followed O'Leary's trail across the Southern Alps. Some literary critics dismiss this kind of information as 'the biographical fallacy'. I should concentrate on the text in front of me, they sternly warn, and not make digressions on the circumstances of the authors. Perhaps they're right, but I remain incorrigibly and unrepentantly curious about the connections between writers' lives and their public utterances. Most readers, I suspect, are of a similar persuasion.

The poet who appears most often in the book is James K. Baxter, with six contributions: 'High Country Weather', 'Poem in the Matukituki Valley', 'The Maori Jesus', 'The Ballad of Calvary Street', 'Farmhand', 'He Waiata mo Te Kare'. The nearest contender is Alfred, Lord Tennyson, with four entries. Baxter's predominance is hardly surprising, for he was astonishingly prolific throughout his brief life. Even with white space kept to a minimum, the hefty, posthumously published volume of his *Collected Poems* runs to more than 600 pages – and there's reputed to be twice as much verse left uncollected. Ranging in time from his teenage years to his late incarnation as a ragged hippie on the banks of the Whanganui River, the half-dozen poems selected here make a great mini-anthology, capturing Baxter in his various moods, alternately disconsolate, reverential, savage, witty and tender.

In all, 25 of our hundred favourite poems are local. That's a sensible proportion, I reckon – enough to demonstrate our pride in New Zealand achievements but not so many that we lose our sense of decency and perspective. While cheering on the Kiwi versifiers, we recognise that Shakespeare, Wordsworth, Keats, Tennyson, Yeats and Auden wrote some good stuff too.

What impresses me most about our selection, however, is its sense of fair play and lack of snobbery. Whereas the British could only bring themselves to include Spike Milligan's 'On the Ning Nang Nong', Pam Ayres's 'Oh, I Wish I'd Looked After Me Teeth' and Lewis Carroll's 'The Walrus and the Carpenter' in the anthology of specifically comic verse, we bung them straight into our main grouping. We're not overly concerned with literary reputations either. If we like a poem, we vote for it, even if the author is not particularly well-known.

As well as Tuwhare, Glover and Baxter, there are other distinguished names among the New Zealand contingent in our list: Margaret Mahy (with her glorious tongue-twister 'Bubble Trouble'), Bub Bridger, Ruth Dallas, Brian Turner (with an exquisite love poem – not a genre with which he is generally associated), Bill Manhire (with an Antarctic offering specially written for Sir Edmund Hillary to recite), Sam Hunt, Lauris Edmond, Glenn Colquhoun. The sixth slot in our hundred, however, goes to Christchurch schoolgirl Charlotte Trevella with her deeply felt poem 'A Drowning'. Porirua poet Trudi Sutcliffe, who is yet to publish a collection of her work, also makes the top ten (at number eight) with 'Counting the Cent', a terrific evocation of Saturday morning markets that I had not read prior to its appearance in this anthology. Another schoolgirl, 13-year-old Aucklander Jennifer Hutchison, takes the 26th slot with 'Misty Tree', thereby beating such time-honoured international stalwarts as 'The Rime of the Ancient Mariner' and 'The Charge of the Light Brigade'. Good on you, Jennifer!

I'm delighted to see L.E. Scott among the preferred hundred too. Lew hails from deep in the American South (Cordele, Georgia, to be precise), but having lived in New Zealand since the early 1970s he can fairly be deemed one of us. Hitherto, however, Kiwi anthologists have been slow to acknowledge him. His contribution to this book, 'Throughout Life', is an unimprovable little gem. Lew, my buddy, if the votes are any indication, you have exceeded your target of 'six friendships'. At your funeral – and may this event be many decades hence – instead of 'six strangers complaining about the heavy load', there might well be a punch-up among potential pallbearers fighting for the honour.

I'm also pleased that New Zealand poetry-lovers have found a place in their hearts for dear old Thomas Bracken, who squeaks in at number 99. Although complaints are legion about the 'triple-star' wretchedness of his lyrics to 'God Defend New Zealand', he nevertheless deserves some recognition as one of the early New Zealand pioneers to have a crack at scaling Mount Parnassus. It's not the national anthem that gains him a place here anyhow, but one of his more melancholy musings on life's perplexity: 'Not understood! How many breasts are aching/ For lack of sympathy! Ah! day by day/ How many cheerless, lonely hearts are breaking!/ How many noble spirits pass away,/ Not understood.'

Sterling fare – the 'Eleanor Rigby' of the 1890s! I can't resist pointing out, though, for the benefit of those who don't already know, that A.R.D. Fairburn wrote an entertaining parody of this poem, which he addressed to 'the Secret Brotherhood, with a bouquet of ragwort and bracken'. My favourite verse, which lifts a few ideas from Wordsworth's 'Resolution and Independence', goes like this: 'Not understood. Despondency and madness/ Attend us as communications fail;/ We poets in our youth begin in gladness,/ But end in Paul's or Whitcombe's Christmas sale,/ Not understood.'[1]

Yet Bracken's original touches on something real enough to withstand Fairburn's clever satirical thrusts. Much the same might be said of some of the English poets in this book, such as Alfred Noyes, Walter de la Mare, W.H. Davis, John Masefield, G.K. Chesterton, W.E. Henley and, indeed, A.E. Housman. I majored in English literature at university and was always particularly keen on the poetry options, but none of the writers I have just mentioned featured in any of the courses I took. If lecturers bothered to mention them at all, it was generally with a sneer. These were the reactionary duffers, they suggested, who stood in the way of progressive poetics at the end of the nineteenth century and the beginning of the twentieth.

Yet the so-called duffers and obstructionists stubbornly refuse to depart for oblivion. Going by the nominations of

[1] 'Not Understood', *Collected Poems*, ARD Fairburn, Pegasus: 1966)

New Zealand poetry enthusiasts, their literary stock is currently riding higher than that of the Modernists (Eliot excepted), who supposedly replaced them forever. 'The Highwayman' remains a peculiarly thrilling – and rather kinky – read. 'The Listeners' can still raise goose pimples. Once introduced to the phrase, who (except, perhaps, the much-lampooned Prince of Wales) can forget Chesterton's 'ears like errant wings'? Or Masefield's beguilingly mysterious 'quinquereme of Nineveh'? (A quinquereme is an ancient kind of boat – a galley with five banks of oars. When I was young I confused Nineveh with Nivea and thought that Masefield was referring to a gooey upmarket hand-lotion. But I still loved the assonantal ring of the syllables.)

Like many New Zealanders, I have been familiar since childhood with some of the more celebrated chestnuts presented by Noyes, de la Mare, Davis, Masefield, Chesterton and Henley. Having never formally studied these writers, however, I knew little about their careers. Fallacious old biography-hound that I am, in recent weeks I have enjoyed reading the entries on them in Wikipedia and literary guides. They are far more complex figures than I had previously imagined.

Take Henley, for instance. Yes, viewed from some angles he was undoubtedly a reactionary, staunchly Tory, unremittingly imperialist. Yet he was also a supporter of Whistler, one of the most avant-garde artists of his era. In his capacity as a magazine editor, he published important early work by Hardy, Yeats and Henry James. He wrote impressionistic free verse as well as lyrics in traditional metre. 'Invictus', the poem of his that we New Zealanders especially like, was written from a hospital bed in 1875, when Henley was 26. Afflicted with tuberculosis of the bone as a teenager, he had his left leg amputated at the knee. He was fighting in 1875 to save his other leg. That goes a long way, I think, towards explaining the peculiarly stroppy and defiant tone of 'Invictus'. Henley was a friend of Robert Louis Stevenson, who is said to have based the character of Long John Silver on him. It improves 'Invictus' for me if I imagine Long John as the speaker, with his parrot on his shoulder repeating key phrases. 'Bloody but unbowed, me hearties, bloody but unbowed!'

As well as my biographical ferreting, I have been struggling lately to recall lessons on the rudiments of English metre that Reg Lockstone imparted with such flair to my classmates and me in the 1960s. I jettisoned this knowledge as hopelessly arcane and redundant when I became a university student in the 1970s. Free verse, I believed back then, had rendered traditional forms obsolete. In the jargon of the time, 'the word had been freed'. Nowadays I am nowhere near as confident that free verse won't ultimately be regarded as a temporary aberration. Though by no means all, a persuasive majority of the poems in this book rhyme and swing along to a steady beat. In the hands of such deft practitioners as Wordsworth, Auden, Glover and Mahy, rhythmic patterns are entrancing. Rhyme can deliver such a satisfying sense of closure.

Let's get a little technical for a moment. 'If—' emerged decisively as the most popular poem in the British survey and in our own poll it appears (at number three) as the highest-ranking effort by a non-Kiwi. Listen to the rhythm. 'If—' is written in regular 'da-dum da-dum' iambic pentameter, except that all the odd-numbered lines from the first to thirty-first end in an extra unstressed syllable ('about you', 'doubt you', 'waiting', 'hating' etc). In Victorian and Edwardian times these were known as 'feminine endings'. I wonder to what extent Kipling was aware of this. Did he realise that his advice on manliness was so infused with femininity? Possibly. Behind the tub-thumping and occasional jingoism, Kipling was a complicated personality, trickier and even more contradictory than Henley. Look at the gleeful lawlessness of his second entry in this book, 'A Smuggler's Song': 'Brandy for the Parson,/ 'Baccy for the Clerk.' An imperialist? Sure. But sometimes he enjoyed the spectacle of the empire striking back.

The British, by the way, did not like 'A Smuggler's Song' as much as we do. It was not in their top hundred. Neither was 'Invictus'. This raises the question of how much our poetic preferences tell us about the national psyche (if, indeed, such a thing exists — some would deny it). Is it because we are a proud people who nevertheless have a bit of an inferiority complex about our size and remote location that we warm to the defiant, head-held-high poems of Henley and Maya Angelou? Is it because we can't bear to be overly regulated that we admire 'A Smuggler's Song' and rate 'The Highwayman' so highly? Is it because we regard the signing of the Treaty of Waitangi in 1840 as the beginning of more or less everything, that we are reluctant to acknowledge overseas poems written more than 50 years before this date, unless they are Shakespeare sonnets? (Gray's 'Elegy' is the only other exception.) Of course, with one hundred poems to work with, it's possible to take many different approaches and compile a great variety of competing psychological charts.

From some perspectives, one hundred seems a large number. From others, it's quite small. Many excellent poems were nominated that were unable to be accommodated in these pages. Sometimes the compilers thought, 'Ah, if only more people were aware of this poem, it would romp home.' One proud father from North Canterbury sent in a sensitive intimation of mortality composed by his 11-year-old son. Because I know other readers will be as touched by it as I was, I am sneaking it in as part of the preface:

LIAM MCKINSTRY 1994–

THE BEACH

As I walk along the beach,
the wind whips my face,
the sand bites my legs.
Seaweed and driftwood advance on the dunes.
It seems as if the whole sea is washing up.
Waves smash, smash, smash
like powerful hydraulic rams pounding the shore.
Gulls screech and scrag each other, trying to impress.
I can taste the salt in the air.
The marram grass dances in the wind.
I come across a dead shag –
its body is like a clump of damp seaweed,
its feathers shuffled in the heavy wind.
Its neck was twisted and bent unnaturally.
Something about that still, lifeless creature jolts and churns my insides.
The tumbling of marbles pulls me away.
I look up at the towering gulls.
The grey-painted sky falls drip, drip, drip,
Soaking me to the bone.
The tide comes in, licking up the soft gold sand.
I look back and see my footprints fading.
I see the shag I stand there transfixed.
This chilling sensation comes over me.
As I stand I think why –
that could be anything, anyone, anywhere.
Someone could be lying stone dead beneath a clump of seaweed,
never to be found.
The rain still falls and I snap back to reality.
As I lie in bed that night,
I listen to the waves as they fight the moon's grasp.

HONE TUWHARE 1922–

RAIN

I can hear you making
small holes in the silence
rain

If I were deaf
the pores of my skin
would open to you
and shut

And I should know you
by the lick of you
if I were blind:

the steady drum-roll
sound you make
when the wind drops

the something
special smell of you
when the sun cakes
the ground

But if I should not
hear
smell or feel or see you

you would still
define me
disperse me
wash over me
rain

DENIS GLOVER 1912–80
THE MAGPIES

When Tom and Elizabeth took the farm
The bracken made their bed,
And *Quardle oodle ardle wardle doodle*
The magpies said.

Tom's hand was strong to the plough
Elizabeth's lips were red,
And *Quardle oodle ardle wardle doodle*
The magpies said.

Year in year out they worked
While the pines grew overhead,
And *Quardle oodle ardle wardle doodle*
The magpies said.

But all the beautiful crops soon went
To the mortgage-man instead,
And *Quardle oodle ardle wardle doodle*
The magpies said.

Elizabeth is dead now (it's years ago);
Old Tom went light in the head;
And *Quardle oodle ardle wardle doodle*
The magpies said.

The farm's still there. Mortgage corporations
Couldn't give it away.
And *Quardle oodle ardle wardle doodle*
The magpies say.

RUDYARD KIPLING 1865–1936

IF –

'Brother Square-Toes' – *Rewards and Fairies*

If you can keep your head when all about you
    Are losing theirs and blaming it on you,
If you can trust yourself when all men doubt you,
    But make allowance for their doubting too;
If you can wait and not be tired by waiting,
    Or being lied about, don't deal in lies,
Or being hated, don't give way to hating,
    And yet don't look too good, nor talk too wise:

If you can dream – and not make dreams your master;
    If you can think – and not make thoughts your aim;
If you can meet with Triumph and Disaster
    And treat those two imposters just the same;
If you can bear to hear the truth you've spoken
    Twisted by knaves to make a trap for fools,
Or watch the things you gave your life to, broken,
    And stoop and build 'em up with worn-out tools:

If you can make one heap of all your winnings
    And risk it on one turn of pitch-and-toss,
And lose, and start again at your beginnings
    And never breathe a word about your loss;
If you can force your heart and nerve and sinew
    To serve your turn long after they are gone,
And so hold on when there is nothing in you
    Except the Will which says to them: 'Hold on!'

If you can talk with crowds and keep your virtue,
    Or walk with Kings – nor lose the common touch,
If neither foes nor loving friends can hurt you,
    If all men count with you, but none too much;
If you can fill the unforgiving minute
    With sixty seconds' worth of distance run,
Yours is the Earth and everything that's in it,
    And – which is more – you'll be a Man, my son!

WILLIAM WORDSWORTH 1770–1850
DAFFODILS

I wander'd lonely as a cloud
That floats on high o'er vales and hills,
When all at once I saw a crowd,
A host of golden daffodils,
Beside the lake, beneath the trees
Fluttering and dancing in the breeze.

Continuous as the stars that shine
And twinkle on the milky way,
They stretch'd in never-ending line
Along the margin of a bay:
Ten thousand saw I at a glance
Tossing their heads in sprightly dance.

The waves beside them danced, but they
Out-did the sparkling waves in glee: –
A Poet could not but be gay
In such a jocund company!
I gazed – and gazed – but little thought
What wealth the show to me had brought.

For oft, when on my couch I lie
In vacant or in pensive mood,
They flash upon that inward eye
Which is the bliss of solitude;
And then my heart with pleasure fills
And dances with the daffodils.

ALFRED NOYES 1880–1958

THE HIGHWAYMAN

I

The wind was a torrent of darkness among the gusty trees,
The moon was a ghostly galleon tossed upon cloudy seas,
The road was a ribbon of moonlight over the purple moor,
And the highwayman came riding –
   Riding – riding –
The highwayman came riding, up to the old inn-door.

He'd a French cocked-hat on his forehead, a bunch of lace at his chin,
A coat of claret velvet, and breeches of brown doe-skin;
They fitted with never a wrinkle: his boots were up to the thigh!
And he rode with a jewelled twinkle,
   His pistol butts a-twinkle,
His rapier hilt a-twinkle, under the jewelled sky.

Over the cobbles he clattered and clashed in the dark inn-yard,
And he tapped with his whip on the shutters, but all was
   locked and barred;
He whistled a tune to the window, and who should be waiting there
But the landlord's black-eyed daughter,
   Bess, the landlord's daughter,
Plaiting a dark red love-knot into her long black hair.

And dark in the old inn-yard a stable-wicket creaked
Where Tim the ostler listened; his face was white and peaked;
His eyes were hollows of madness, his hair like mouldy hay,
But he loved the landlord's daughter,
   The landlord's red-lipped daughter;
Dumb as a dog he listened, and he heard the robber say –

'One kiss, my bonny sweetheart, I'm after a prize to-night,
But I shall be back with the yellow gold before the morning light;
Yet, if they press me sharply, and harry me through the day,
Then look for me by moonlight,
    Watch for me by moonlight,
I'll come to thee by moonlight, though hell should bar the way.'

He rose upright in the stirrups; he scarce could reach her hand,
But she loosened her hair i' the casement! His face burnt like a brand
As the black cascade of perfume came tumbling over his breast;
And he kissed its waves in the moonlight,
    (Oh, sweet black waves in the moonlight!)
Then he tugged at his rein in the moonlight, and galloped away to the west.

II

He did not come in the dawning; he did not come at noon;
And out o' the tawny sunset, before the rise o' the moon,
When the road was a gipsy's ribbon, looping the purple moor,
A red-coat troop came marching –
    Marching – marching –
King George's men came marching, up to the old inn-door.

They said no word to the landlord, they drank his ale instead,
But they gagged his daughter and bound her to the foot of her
    narrow bed;
Two of them knelt at her casement, with muskets at their side!
There was death at every window;
    And hell at one dark window;
For Bess could see, through her casement, the road that *he* would ride.
They had tied her up to attention, with many a sniggering jest;
They had bound a musket beside her, with the barrel beneath her breast!
'Now keep good watch!' and they kissed her.
    She heard the dead man say –
Look for me by moonlight;
    Watch for me by moonlight;
I'll come to thee by moonlight, though hell should bar the way!

She twisted her hands behind her; but all the knots held good!
She writhed her hands till her fingers were wet with sweat or blood!
They stretched and strained in the darkness, and the hours crawled by
    like years,
Till, now, on the stroke of midnight,
    Cold, on the stroke of midnight,
The tip of one finger touched it! The trigger at least was hers!

The tip of one finger touched it; she strove no more for the rest!
Up, she stood to attention, with the barrel beneath her breast,
She would not risk their hearing; she would not strive again;
For the road lay bare in the moonlight;
    Blank and bare in the moonlight;
And the blood of her veins in the moonlight throbbed to her love's refrain.

Tlot-tlot; tlot-tlot! Had they heard it? The horse-hoofs ringing clear;
Tlot-tlot, tlot-tlot, in the distance? Were they deaf that they did not hear?
Down the ribbon of moonlight, over the brow of the hill,
The highwayman came riding,
    Riding, riding!
The red-coats looked to their priming! She stood up straight and still!

Tlot-tlot, in the frosty silence! *tlot-tlot,* in the echoing night!
Nearer he came and nearer! Her face was like a light!
Her eyes grew wide for a moment; she drew one last deep breath,
Then her finger moved in the moonlight,
    Her musket shattered the moonlight,
Shattered her breast in the moonlight and warned him – with her death.
He turned; he spurred to the westward; he did not know who stood
Bowed, with her head o'er the musket, drenched with her own red blood!
Not till the dawn he heard it, and slowly blanched to hear
How Bess, the landlord's daughter,
    The landlord's black-eyed daughter,
Had watched for her love in the moonlight, and died in the darkness there.

Back, he spurred like a madman, shrieking a curse to the sky,
With the white road smoking behind him and his rapier brandished high!
Blood-red were his spurs i' the golden noon; wine-red was his velvet coat;
When they shot him down on the highway,
Down like a dog on the highway,
And he lay in his blood on the highway, with the bunch of lace at his throat.

And still of a winter's night, they say, when the wind is in the trees,
When the moon is a ghostly galleon tossed upon cloudy seas,
When the road is a ribbon of moonlight over the purple moor,
A highwayman comes riding —
Riding — riding —
A highwayman comes riding, up to the old inn-door.

Over the cobbles he clatters and clangs in the dark inn-yard
And he taps with his whip on the shutters, but all is locked and barred;
He whistles a tune to the window, and who should be waiting there
But the landlord's black-eyed daughter,
Bess, the landlord's daughter,
Plaiting a dark red love-knot into her long black hair.

CHARLOTTE TREVELLA 1992–

A DROWNING

The day
    after
a ship's skeleton
    is drifting
    further
away from land.

Parents
    stand on cliff
    edge
and say;
'last night's storm.
Pity. Some survived
though.
Some.'

At water's
    edge
children help
    the sea sort
through
    flotsam and
wreckage.

Trying on
    waterlogged bonnets and caps
    until parents shout
'Oi! Away from
the dead man's clothes.'

Dawn light brightens.
Tears fall
    like seawater.

ROBERT FROST 1874–1963

THE ROAD NOT TAKEN

Two roads diverged in a yellow wood,
And sorry I could not travel both
And be one traveller, long I stood
And looked down one as far as I could
To where it bent in the undergrowth;

Then took the other, as just as fair,
And having perhaps the better claim,
Because it was grassy and wanted wear;
Though as for that the passing there
Had worn them really about the same,

And both that morning equally lay
In leaves no step had trodden black.
Oh, I kept the first for another day!
Yet knowing how way leads on to way,
I doubted if I should ever come back.

I shall be telling this with a sigh
Somewhere ages and ages hence:
Two roads diverged in a wood, and I –
I took the one less travelled by,
And that has made all the difference.

TRUDI SUTCLIFFE 1972–

COUNTING THE CENT

The time, 5:45am, Saturday Market Day,
Floor is cold. Clothes, shoes thrown on.
Ice wrapped around the car, a slow start.

Pull into the car park Mum and me.
Trucks trekked from Hawke's Bay, sunny Otaki; trailers too.
Standing tall in their fought spot in the city of opportunity.

Babies in backpacks, toddlers pulling stretched fingers,
Woolly heads dodging shapes in the half-light,
Before a trolley slides over a stunned toe.

Hungry teeth biting hot kebabs,
Sniffing the scent of fried Māori bread, German buns.
The sweet coconut bread spoils our dry throats.

A van carries music while dull pots
Clink with china and hula beside an old soda stream.
Books yellow and dusty, finger for hidden classics.

Stall to stall searching, examining.
A megaphone swears he has the cheapest potato,
In the following breath warns a number plate of an approaching ticket.

Another swears he has the cheapest ten-roll toilet paper,
While we crunch on an apple, free due to cunning enterprise,
Then buying a bag as we count every cent.

We head home, arms weighed down, fingers losing feel.
Home to sweet bread, warm kitchen,
Hungry kids waiting.

JAMES K. BAXTER 1926–72

HIGH COUNTRY WEATHER

Alone we are born
   And die alone;
Yet see the red-gold cirrus
   Over snow-mountain shine.

Upon the upland road
   Ride easy, stranger:
Surrender to the sky
   Your heart of anger.

W. H. AUDEN 1907–73

From TWELVE SONGS

IX

Stop all the clocks, cut off the telephone,
Prevent the dog from barking with a juicy bone,
Silence the pianos and with muffled drum
Bring out the coffin, let the mourners come.

Let aeroplanes circle moaning overhead
Scribbling on the sky the message He Is Dead,
Put crêpe bows round the white necks of the public doves,
Let the traffic policemen wear black cotton gloves.

He was my North, my South, my East and West,
My working week and my Sunday rest,
My noon, my midnight, my talk, my song;
I thought that love would last for ever: I was wrong.

The stars are not wanted now: put out every one;
Pack up the moon and dismantle the sun;
Pour away the ocean and sweep up the wood.
For nothing now can ever come to any good.

HONE TUWHARE 1922–

NO ORDINARY SUN

Tree let your arms fall:
raise them not sharply in supplication
to the bright enhaloed cloud.
Let your arms lack toughness and
resilience for this is no mere axe
to blunt, nor fire to smother.

Your sap shall not rise again
to the moon's pull.
No more incline a deferential head
to the wind's talk, or stir
to the tickle of coursing rain.

Your former shagginess shall not be
wreathed with the delightful flight
of birds nor shield
nor cool the ardour of unheeding
lovers from the monstrous sun.

Tree let your naked arms fall
nor extend vain entreaties to the radiant ball.
This is no gallant monsoon's flash,
no dashing trade wind's blast.
The fading green of your magic
emanations shall not make pure again
these polluted skies... for this
is no ordinary sun.

O tree
in the shadowless mountains
the white plains and
the drab sea floor
your end at last is written.

DYLAN THOMAS 1914–53

DO NOT GO GENTLE INTO THAT GOOD NIGHT

Do not go gentle into that good night,
Old age should burn and rave at close of day;
Rage, rage against the dying of the light.

Though wise men at their end know dark is right,
Because their words had forked no lightning they
Do not go gentle into that good night.

Good men, the last wave by, crying how bright
Their frail deeds might have danced in a green bay,
Rage, rage against the dying of the light.

Wild men who caught and sang the sun in flight,
And learn, too late, they grieved it on its way,
Do not go gentle into that good night.

Grave men, near death, who see with blinding sight
Blind eyes could blaze like meteors and be gay,
Rage, rage against the dying of the light.

And you, my father, there on the sad height,
Curse, bless, me now with your fierce tears, I pray.
Do not go gentle into that good night.
Rage, rage against the dying of the light.

EDWARD LEAR 1812–88

THE OWL AND THE PUSSY-CAT

The Owl and the Pussy-Cat went to sea
   In a beautiful pea-green boat.
They took some honey, and plenty of money
   Wrapped up in a five-pound note.
The Owl looked up to the stars above,
   And sang to a small guitar,
'O lovely Pussy! O Pussy, my love,
What a beautiful Pussy you are,
     You are,
     You are!
What a beautiful Pussy you are!'

Pussy said to the Owl, 'You elegant fowl!
   How charmingly sweet you sing!
O let us be married! too long we have tarried:
   But what shall we do for a ring?'
They sailed away, for a year and a day,
   To the land where the Bong-Tree grows,
And there in a wood a Piggy-wig stood,
With a ring at the end of his nose,
     His nose,
     His nose!
With a ring at the end of his nose.

'Dear Pig, are you willing to sell for one shilling
   Your ring?' Said the Piggy, 'I will.'
So they took it away, and were married next day
   By the Turkey who lives on the hill.
They dined on mince, and slices of quince,
   Which they ate with a runcible spoon;
And hand in hand, on the edge of the sand
They danced by the light of the moon,
     The moon,
     The moon,
They danced by the light of the moon.

WILLIAM BLAKE 1757–1827

THE TYGER

Tyger! Tyger! burning bright
In the forests of the night,
What immortal hand or eye
Could frame thy fearful symmetry?

In what distant deeps or skies
Burnt the fire of thine eyes?
On what wings dare he aspire?
What the hand dare seize the fire?

And what shoulder, & what art,
Could twist the sinews of thy heart?
And when thy heart began to beat,
What dread hand? & what dread feet?

What the hammer? what the chain?
In what furnace was thy brain?
What the anvil? what dread grasp
Dare its deadly terrors clasp?

When the stars threw down their spears,
And water'd heaven with their tears,
Did he smile his work to see?
Did he who made the Lamb make thee?

Tyger! Tyger! burning bright
In the forests of the night,
What immortal hand or eye,
Dare frame thy fearful symmetry?

SPIKE MILLIGAN 1918–2002

ON THE NING NANG NONG

On the Ning Nang Nong
Where the Cows go Bong!
And the Monkeys all say Boo!
There's a Nong Nang Ning
Where the trees go Ping!
And the tea pots Jibber Jabber Joo.
On the Nong Ning Nang
All the mice go Clang!
And you just can't catch 'em when they do!
So it's Ning Nang Nong!
Cows go Bong!
Nong Nang Ning!
Trees go Ping!
Nong Ning Nang!
The mice go Clang!
What a noisy place to belong,
Is the Ning Nang
    Ning Nang Nong!!

THE LOVE SONG OF J. ALFRED PRUFROCK

S'io credessi che mia risposta fosse
a persona che mai tornasse al mondo,
questa fiamma staria senza più scosse.
Ma per ciò che giammai di questo fondo
non tornò vivo alcun, s'i'odo il vero,
senza tema d'infamia ti rispondo.

Let us go then, you and I,
When the evening is spread out against the sky
Like a patient etherised upon a table;
Let us go, through certain half-deserted streets,
The muttering retreats
Of restless nights in one-night cheap hotels
And sawdust restaurants with oyster-shells:
Streets that follow like a tedious argument
Of insidious intent
To lead you to an overwhelming question …
Oh, do not ask, 'What is it?'
Let us go and make our visit.

In the room the women come and go
Talking of Michelangelo.

The yellow fog that rubs its back upon the window-panes,
The yellow smoke that rubs its muzzle on the window-panes,
Licked its tongue into the corners of the evening,
Lingered upon the pools that stand in drains,
Let fall upon its back the soot that falls from chimneys,
Slipped by the terrace, made a sudden leap,
And seeing that it was a soft October night,
Curled once about the house, and fell asleep.

And indeed there will be time
For the yellow smoke that slides along the street

Rubbing its back upon the window-panes;
There will be time, there will be time
To prepare a face to meet the faces that you meet;
There will be time to murder and create,
And time for all the works and days of hands
That lift and drop a question on your plate;
Time for you and time for me,
And time yet for a hundred indecisions,
And for a hundred visions and revisions,
Before the taking of a toast and tea.

In the room the women come and go
Talking of Michelangelo.

And indeed there will be time
To wonder, 'Do I dare?' and, 'Do I dare?'
Time to turn back and descend the stair,
With a bald spot in the middle of my hair –
(They will say: 'How his hair is growing thin!')
My morning coat, my collar mounting firmly to the chin,
My necktie rich and modest, but asserted by a simple pin –
(They will say: 'But how his arms and legs are thin!')
Do I dare
Disturb the universe?
In a minute there is time
For decisions and revisions which a minute will reverse.

For I have known them all already, known them all –
Have known the evenings, mornings, afternoons,
I have measured out my life with coffee spoons;
I know the voices dying with a dying fall
Beneath the music from a farther room.
     So how should I presume?

And I have known the eyes already, known them all –
The eyes that fix you in a formulated phrase,

And when I am formulated, sprawling on a pin,
When I am pinned and wriggling on the wall,
Then how should I begin
To spit out all the butt-ends of my days and ways?
    And how should I presume?

    And I have known the arms already, known them all –
Arms that are braceleted and white and bare
(But in the lamplight, downed with light brown hair!)
Is it perfume from a dress
That makes me so digress?
Arms that lie along a table, or wrap about a shawl.
    And should I then presume?
    And how should I begin?

          . . . . .

    Shall I say, I have gone at dusk through narrow streets
And watched the smoke that rises from the pipes
Of lonely men in shirt-sleeves, leaning out of windows? ...

    I should have been a pair of ragged claws
Scuttling across the floors of silent seas.

          . . . . .

    And the afternoon, the evening, sleeps so peacefully!
Smoothed by long fingers,
Asleep ... tired ... or it malingers,
Stretched on the floor, here beside you and me.
Should I, after tea and cakes and ices,
Have the strength to force the moment to its crisis?
But though I have wept and fasted, wept and prayed,
Though I have seen my head (grown slightly bald)
    brought in upon a platter,
I am no prophet – and here's no great matter;

I have seen the moment of my greatness flicker,
and I have seen the eternal Footman hold my coat, and
    snicker,
And in short, I was afraid.

    And would it have been worth it, after all,
After the cups, the marmalade, the tea,
Among the porcelain, among some talk of you and me,
Would it have been worth while,
To have bitten off the matter with a smile,
To have squeezed the universe into a ball
To roll it toward some overwhelming question,
To say: 'I am Lazarus, come from the dead,
Come back to tell you all, I shall tell you all' –
If one, settling a pillow by her head,
    Should say: 'That is not what I meant at all.
    That is not it, at all.'

    And would it have been worth it, after all,
Would it have been worth while,
After the sunsets and the dooryards and the sprinkled
    streets,
After the novels, after the teacups, after the skirts that
    trail along the floor –
And this, and so much more? –
It is impossible to say just what I mean!
But as if a magic lantern threw the nerves in patterns on a
    screen:
Would it have been worth while
If one, settling a pillow or throwing off a shawl,
And turning toward the window, should say:
    'That is not it at all,
    That is not what I meant, at all.'

    . . . . .

No! I am not Prince Hamlet, nor was meant to be;
Am an attendant lord, one that will do
To swell a progress, start a scene or two,
Advise the prince; no doubt, an easy tool,
Deferential, glad to be of use,
Politic, cautious, and meticulous;
Full of high sentence, but a bit obtuse;
At times, indeed, almost ridiculous —
Almost, at times, the Fool.

I grow old ... I grow old ...
I shall wear the bottoms of my trousers rolled.

Shall I part my hair behind? Do I dare to eat a peach?
I shall wear white flannel trousers, and walk upon the beach.
I have heard the mermaids singing, each to each.

I do not think that they will sing to me.

I have seen them riding seaward on the waves
Combing the white hair of the waves blown back
When the wind blows the water white and black.

We have lingered in the chambers of the sea
By sea-girls wreathed with seaweed red and brown
Till human voices wake us, and we drown.

WILLIAM BUTLER YEATS 1865–1939

THE LAKE ISLE OF INNISFREE

I will arise and go now, and go to Innisfree,
And a small cabin build there, of clay and wattles made:
Nine bean-rows will I have there, a hive for the honey-bee,
And live alone in the bee-loud glade.

And I shall have some peace there, for peace comes dropping slow,
Dropping from the veils of the morning to where the cricket sings;
There midnight's all a glimmer, and noon a purple glow,
And evening full of the linnet's wings.

I will arise and go now, for always night and day
I hear lake water lapping with low sounds by the shore;
While I stand on the roadway, or on the pavements grey,
I hear it in the deep heart's core.

JABBERWOCKY

'Twas brillig, and the slithy toves
    Did gyre and gimble in the wabe;
All mimsy were the borogoves,
    And the mome raths outgrabe.

'Beware the Jabberwock, my son!
    The jaws that bite, the claws that catch!
Beware the Jubjub bird, and shun
    The frumious Bandersnatch!'

He took his vorpal sword in hand:
    Long time the manxome foe he sought –
So rested he by the Tumtum tree,
    And stood awhile in thought.

And as in uffish thought he stood,
    The Jabberwock, with eyes of flame,
Came whiffling through the tulgey wood,
    And burbled as it came!

One, two! One, two! And through and through
    The vorpal blade went snicker-snack!
He left it dead, and with its head
    He went galumphing back.

'And hast thou slain the Jabberwock?
    Come to my arms, my beamish boy!
O frabjous day! Callooh! Callay!'
    He chortled in his joy.

'Twas brillig, and the slithy toves
    Did gyre and gimble in the wabe;
All mimsy were the borogoves,
    And the mome raths outgrabe.

WILLIAM BUTLER YEATS 1865–1939

HE WISHES FOR THE CLOTHS OF HEAVEN

Had I the heavens' embroidered cloths,
Enwrought with golden and silver light,
The blue and the dim and the dark cloths
Of night and light and the half-light,
I would spread the cloths under your feet:
But I, being poor, have only my dreams;
I have spread my dreams under your feet;
Tread softly because you tread on my dreams.

CHRISTINA ROSSETTI 1830–94

REMEMBER

Remember me when I am gone away,
    Gone far away into the silent land;
    When you can no more hold me by the hand,
Nor I half turn to go yet turning stay.
Remember me when no more day by day
    You tell me of our future that you planned:
    Only remember me; you understand
It will be late to counsel then or pray.
Yet if you should forget me for a while
    And afterwards remember, do not grieve:
    For if the darkness and corruption leave
    A vestige of the thoughts that once I had,
Better by far you should forget and smile
    Than that you should remember and be sad.

ALFRED, LORD TENNYSON 1809–92

CROSSING THE BAR

Sunset and evening star,
 And one clear call for me!
And may there be no moaning of the bar,
 When I put out to sea,

But such a tide as moving seems asleep,
 Too full for sound and foam,
When that which drew from out the boundless deep
 Turns again home.

Twilight and evening bell,
 And after that the dark!
And may there be no sadness of farewell,
 When I embark;

For though from out our bourne of Time and Place
 The flood may bear me far,
I hope to see my Pilot face to face
 When I have crost the bar.

JENNY JOSEPH 1932—

WARNING

When I am an old woman I shall wear purple
With a red hat which doesn't go, and doesn't suit me.
And I shall spend my pension on brandy and summer gloves
And satin sandals, and say we've no money for butter.
I shall sit down on the pavement when I'm tired
And gobble up samples in shops and press alarm bells
And run my stick along the public railings
And make up for the sobriety of my youth.
I shall go out in my slippers in the rain
And pick the flowers in other people's gardens
And learn to spit.

You can wear terrible shirts and grow more fat
And eat three pounds of sausages at a go
Or only bread and pickle for a week
And hoard pens and pencils and beermats and things in boxes.

But now we must have clothes that keep us dry
And pay our rent and not swear in the street
And set a good example for the children.
We must have friends to dinner and read the papers.

But maybe I ought to practise a little now?
So people who know me are not too shocked and surprised
When suddenly I am old, and start to wear purple.

PERCY BYSSHE SHELLEY 1792–1822
OZYMANDIAS

I met a traveller from an antique land
Who said: Two vast and trunkless legs of stone
Stand in the desert. Near them on the sand,
Half sunk, a shatter'd visage lies, whose frown
And wrinkled lip and sneer of cold command
Tell that its sculptor well those passions read
Which yet survive, stamp'd on these lifeless things,
The hand that mock'd them and the heart that fed;
And on the pedestal these words appear:
'My name is Ozymandias, king of kings:
Look on my works, ye Mighty, and despair!'
Nothing beside remains. Round the decay
Of that colossal wreck, boundless and bare,
The lone and level sands stretch far away.

ALFRED, LORD TENNYSON 1809–92

THE LADY OF SHALOTT

PART I

On either side the river lie
Long fields of barley and of rye,
That clothe the wold and meet the sky;
And thro' the field the road runs by
      To many-tower'd Camelot;
And up and down the people go,
Gazing where the lilies blow
Round an island there below,
      The island of Shalott.

Willows whiten, aspens quiver,
Little breezes dusk and shiver
Thro' the wave that runs for ever
By the island in the river
      Flowing down to Camelot.
Four grey walls, and four grey towers,
Overlook a space of flowers,
And the silent isle imbowers
      The Lady of Shalott.

By the margin, willow-veil'd,
Slide the heavy barges trail'd
By slow horses; and unhail'd
The shallop flitteth silken-sail'd
      Skimming down to Camelot:
But who hath seen her wave her hand?
Or at the casement seen her stand?
Or is she known in all the land,
      The Lady of Shalott?

Only reapers, reaping early
In among the bearded barley,
Hear a song that echoes cheerly
From the river winding clearly,
      Down to tower'd Camelot:
And by the moon the reaper weary,
Piling sheaves in uplands airy,
Listening, whispers ''Tis the fairy
      Lady of Shalott.'

PART II

There she weaves by night and day
A magic web with colours gay.
She has heard a whisper say,
A curse is on her if she stay
      To look down to Camelot.
She knows not what the curse may be,
And so she weaveth steadily,
And little other care hath she,
      The Lady of Shalott.

And moving thro' a mirror clear
That hangs before her all the year,
Shadows of the world appear.
There she sees the highway near
      Winding down to Camelot:
There the river eddy whirls,
And there the surly village-churls,
And the red cloaks of market girls,
      Pass onward from Shalott.

Sometimes a troop of damsels glad,
An abbot on an ambling pad,
Sometimes a curly shepherd-lad,
Or long-hair'd page in crimson clad,

Goes by to tower'd Camelot;
And sometimes thro' the mirror blue
The knights come riding two and two:
She hath no loyal knight and true,
     The Lady of Shalott.

But in her web she still delights
To weave the mirror's magic sights,
For often thro' the silent nights
A funeral, with plumes and lights,
     And music, went to Camelot:
Or when the moon was overhead,
Came two young lovers lately wed;
'I am half sick of shadows,' said
     The Lady of Shalott.

PART III

A bow-shot from her bower-eaves,
He rode between the barley-sheaves,
The sun came dazzling thro' the leaves,
And flamed upon the brazen greaves
     Of bold Sir Lancelot.
A red-cross knight for ever kneel'd
To a lady in his shield,
That sparkled on the yellow field,
     Beside remote Shalott.

The gemmy bridle glitter'd free,
Like to some branch of stars we see
Hung in the golden Galaxy.
The bridle bells rang merrily
     As he rode down to Camelot:
And from his blazon'd baldric slung
A mighty silver bugle hung,
And as he rode his armour rung,
     Beside remote Shalott.

All in the blue unclouded weather
Thick-jewell'd shone the saddle-leather,
The helmet and the helmet-feather
Burn'd like one burning flame together,
　　　As he rode down to Camelot.
As often thro' the purple night,
Below the starry clusters bright,
Some bearded meteor, trailing light,
　　　Moves over still Shalott.

His broad clear brow in sunlight glow'd;
On burnish'd hooves his war-horse trode;
From underneath his helmet flow'd
His coal-black curls as on he rode,
　　　As he rode down to Camelot.
From the bank and from the river
He flash'd into the crystal mirror,
'Tirra lirra,' by the river
　　　Sang Sir Lancelot.

She left the web, she left the loom,
She made three paces thro' the room,
She saw the water-lily bloom,
She saw the helmet and the plume,
　　　She look'd down to Camelot.
Out flew the web and floated wide;
The mirror crack'd from side to side;
'The curse is come upon me,' cried
　　　The Lady of Shalott.

PART IV

In the stormy east-wind straining,
The pale yellow woods were waning,
The broad stream in his banks complaining,
Heavily the low sky raining

Over tower'd Camelot;
Down she came and found a boat
Beneath a willow left afloat,
And round about the prow she wrote
  The Lady of Shalott.

And down the river's dim expanse —
Like some bold seer in a trance,
Seeing all his own mischance —
With a glassy countenance
  Did she look to Camelot.
And at the closing of the day
She loosed the chain, and down she lay;
The broad stream bore her far away,
  The Lady of Shalott.

Lying, robed in snowy white
That loosely flew to left and right —
The leaves upon her falling light —
Thro' the noises of the night
  She floated down to Camelot:
And as the boat-head wound along
The willowy hills and fields among,
They heard her singing her last song.
  The Lady of Shalott.

Heard a carol, mournful, holy,
Chanted loudly, chanted lowly,
Till her blood was frozen slowly,
And her eyes were darken'd wholly,
  Turn'd to tower'd Camelot.
For ere she reach'd upon the tide
The first house by the water-side,
Singing in her song she died
  The Lady of Shalott.

Under tower and balcony,
By garden-wall and gallery,
A gleaming shape she floated by,
Dead-pale between the houses high,
　　　Silent into Camelot.
Out upon the wharfs they came,
Knight and burgher, lord and dame.
And round the prow they read her name,
　　　The Lady of Shalott.

Who is this? and what is here?
And in the lighted palace near
Died the sound of royal cheer;
And they cross'd themselves for fear,
　　　All the knights at Camelot:
But Lancelot mused a little space;
He said. 'She has a lovely face;
God in his mercy lend her grace.
　　　The Lady of Shalott.'

MARGARET MAHY 1936—

BUBBLE TROUBLE

Little Mabel blew a bubble and it caused a lot of trouble...
Such a lot of bubble trouble in a bibble-bobble way.
For it broke away from Mabel as it bobbed across the table,
Where it bobbled over Baby, and it wafted him away.

The baby didn't quibble. He began to smile and dribble,
For he liked the wibble-wobble of the bubble in the air.
But Mabel ran for cover as the bubble bobbed above her,
And she shouted out for Mother who was putting up her hair.

At the sudden cry of trouble, Mother took off at the double,
For the squealing left her reeling...made her terrified and tense,
Saw the bubble for a minute, with the baby bobbing in it,
As it bibbled by the letter-box and bobbed across the fence.

In her garden, Chrysta Gribble had begun to cry and cavil
At her lazy brother, Greville, reading novels in his bed.
But she bellowed, 'Gracious, Greville!' and she grovelled on the gravel,
When the baby in the bubble bibble-bobbled overhead.

In a garden folly, Tybal, and his jolly mother, Sybil,
Sat and played a game of Scrabble, shouting shrilly as they scored.
But they both began to babble and to scrobble with the Scrabble
As the baby in the bubble bibble-bobbled by the board.

Then crippled Mr Copple and his wife (a crabby couple),
Set out arm in arm to hobble and to squabble down the lane.
But the baby in the bubble turned their hobble to a joggle
As they raced away like rockets...and they've never limped again.

Even feeble Mrs Threeble in a muddle with her needle
(Matching pink and purple patches for a pretty patchwork quilt),
When her older sister told her, tossed the quilt across her shoulder,
As she set off at a totter in her tattered tartan kilt.

At the shops a busy rabble met to gossip and to gabble,
Started gibbering and goggling as the bubble bobbled by.
Mother, hand in hand with Mabel, flew as fast as she was able,
Full of trouble lest the bubble burst or vanish in the sky.

After them came Greville Gribble in his nightshirt with his novel
(All about a haunted hovel) held on high above his head,
Followed by his sister, Chrysta (though her boots had made a blister),
Then came Tybal, pulling Sybil, with the Scrabble for a sled.

After them the Copple couple came cavorting at the double,
Then a jogger (quite a slogger) joined the crowd who called and coughed.
Up above the puzzled people – up towards the chapel steeple –
Rose the bubble (with the baby) slowly lifting up aloft.

There was such a flum-a-diddle (Mabel huddled in the middle),
Canon Dapple left the chapel, followed by the chapel choir.
And the treble singer, Abel, threw an apple core at Mabel,
As the baby in the bubble bobbled up a little higher.

Oh, they giggled and they goggled until all their brains were boggled,
As the baby in the bubble rose above the little town.
'With the problem let us grapple,' murmured kindly Canon Dapple,
'And the problem we must grapple with is bringing baby down.

Now, let Mabel stand on Abel, who could stand in turn on Tybal,
Who could stand on Greville Gribble, who could stand upon the wall,
While the people from the shop'll stand to catch them if they topple,
Then perhaps they'll reach the bubble, saving baby from a fall.'

But Abel, though a treble, was a rascal and a rebel,
Fond of getting into trouble when he didn't have to sing.
Pushing quickly through the people, Abel clambered up the steeple
With nefarious intentions and a pebble in his sling!

Abel quietly aimed the pebble past the steeple of the chapel,
At the baby in the bubble wibble-wobbling way up there.
And the pebble *burst* the bubble! So the future seemed to fizzle
For the baby boy who grizzled as he tumbled through the air.

What a moment for a mother as her infant plunged above her!
There were groans and gasps and gargles from the horror-stricken crowd.
Sibyl said, 'Upon my honour, *there's* a baby who's a goner!'
And Chrysta hissed with emphasis, 'It shouldn't be allowed!'

But Mabel, Tybal, Greville and the jogger (christened Neville)
Didn't quiver, didn't quaver, didn't drivel, shrivel, wilt.
But as one they made a swivel, and with action (firm but civil),
They divested Mrs Threeble of her pretty patchwork quilt.

Oh, what calculated catchwork! Baby bounced into the patchwork,
Where his grizzles turned to giggles and to wriggles of delight!
And the people stared dumbfounded, as he bobbled and rebounded,
Till the baby boy was grounded and his mother held him tight.

And the people there still prattle – there is lots of tittle-tattle –
For they glory in the story, young and old folk, gold and grey,
Of how wicked treble Abel tripled trouble with his pebble,
But how Mabel (and some others) saved her brother and the day.

JENNIFER HUTCHISON 1993–

MISTY TREE

The leaves flutter slowly to the ground.
One by one, through the misty heavens,
Forgotten, in the air they are drowned.

Until all but a few cling to the tree.
Battered by wind, they know they must leave,
And rest on the grass for all eternity.

BUB BRIDGER 1924–

WILD DAISIES

If you love me
Bring me flowers
Wild daisies
Clutched in your fist
Like a torch
No orchids or roses
Or carnations
No florist's bow
Just daisies
Steal them
Risk your life for them
Up the sharp hills
In the teeth of the wind
If you love me
Bring me daisies
Wild daisies
That I will cram
In a bright vase
And marvel at

JAMES K. BAXTER 1926–72

POEM IN THE MATUKITUKI VALLEY

Some few yards from the hut the standing beeches
Let fall their dead limbs, overgrown
With feathered moss and filigree of bracken.
The rotted wood splits clean and hard
Close-grained to the driven axe, with sound of water
Sibilant falling and high nested birds.

In winter blind with snow; but in full summer
The forest blanket sheds its cloudy pollen
And cloaks a range in undevouring fire.
Remote the land's heart. Though the wild scrub cattle
Acclimatized, may learn
Shreds of her purpose, or the taloned kea.

For those who come as I do, half-aware,
Wading the swollen
Matukituki waist-high in snow water,
And stumbling where the mountains throw their dice
Of boulders huge as houses, or the smoking
Cataract flings its arrows on our path –

For us the land is matrix and destroyer,
Resentful, darkly known
By sunset omens, low words heard in branches;
Or where the red deer lift their innocent heads
Snuffing the wind for danger,
And from our footfall's menace bound in terror.

Three emblems of the heart I carry folded
As charms against flood water, sliding shale:
Pale gentian, lily, and bush orchid.
The peaks too have names to suit their whiteness,
Stargazer and Moonraker,
A sailor's language and a mountaineer's.

And those who sleep in close bags fitfully
Besieged by wind in a snowline bivouac –
The carrion parrot with red underwing
Clangs on the roof by night, and daybreak brings
Raincloud on purple ranges, light reflected
Stainless from crumbling glacier, dazzling snow,

Do they not, clay in that unearthly furnace,
Endure the hermit's peace
And mindless ecstasy? Blue-lipped crevasse
And smooth rock chimney straddling – a communion
With what eludes our net – Leviathan
Stirring to ocean birth our inland waters?

Sky's purity; the altar cloth of snow
On deathly summits laid; or avalanche
That shakes the rough moraine with giant laughter;
Snowplume and whirlwind – what are these
But His flawed mirror who gave the mountain strength
And dwells in holy calm, undying freshness?

Therefore we turn, hiding our souls' dullness
From that too blinding glass: turn to the gentle
Dark of the human daydream, child and wife,
Patience of stone and soil, the lawful city
Where man may live, and no wild trespass
Of what's eternal shake his grave of time.

SAMUEL TAYLOR COLERIDGE 1772–1834
From THE RIME OF THE ANCIENT MARINER

PART I

It is an ancient Mariner,
And he stoppeth one of three.
'By thy long grey beard and glittering eye,
Now wherefore stopp'st thou me?

The Bridegroom's doors are opened wide.
And I am next of kin;
The guests are met, the feast is set:
May'st hear the merry din.'

He holds him with his skinny hand.
'There was a ship,' quoth he.
'Hold off! unhand me, grey-beard loon!'
Eftsoons his hand dropt he.

He holds him with his glittering eye –
The Wedding-Guest stood still.
And listens like a three years' child:
The Mariner hath his will.

The Wedding-Guest sat on a stone:
He cannot choose but hear:
And thus spake on that ancient man.
The bright-eyed Mariner.

'The ship was cheered, the harbour cleared,
Merrily did we drop
Below the kirk, below the hill,
Below the lighthouse top.

The Sun came up upon the left,
Out of the sea came he!
And he shone bright, and on the right
Went down into the sea.

Higher and higher every day,
Till over the mast at noon —'
The Wedding-Guest here beat his breast,
For he heard the loud bassoon.

The bride hath paced into the hall,
Red as a rose is she;
Nodding their heads before her goes
The merry minstrelsy.

The Wedding-Guest he beat his breast,
Yet he cannot choose but hear;
And thus spake on that ancient man,
The bright-eyed Mariner.

'And now the STORM-BLAST came, and he
Was tyrannous and strong:
He struck with his o'ertaking wings,
And chased us south along.

With sloping masts and dipping prow,
As who pursued with yell and blow
Still treads the shadow of his foe,
And forward bends his head,
The ship drove fast, loud roared the blast,
And southward aye we fled.

And now there came both mist and snow,
And it grew wondrous cold:
And ice, mast-high, came floating by,
As green as emerald.

And through the drifts the snowy clifts
Did send a dismal sheen:
Nor shapes of men nor beasts we ken —
The ice was all between.

The ice was here, the ice was there,
The ice was all around:
It cracked and growled, and roared and howled,
Like noises in a swound!

At length did cross an Albatross,
Thorough the fog it came;
As if it had been a Christian soul,
We hailed it in God's name.

It ate the food it ne'er had eat,
And round and round it flew.
The ice did split with a thunder-fit;
The helmsman steered us through!

And a good south wind sprung up behind;
The Albatross did follow,
And every day, for food or play,
Came to the mariner's hollo!

In mist or cloud, on mast or shroud,
It perched for vespers nine;
Whiles all the night, through fog-smoke white,
Glimmered the white Moon-shine.'

'God save thee, ancient Mariner!
From the fiends, that plague thee thus! —
Why look'st thou so?' — 'With my cross-bow
I shot the Albatross.'

JOHN MCCRAE 1872–1918

IN FLANDERS FIELDS

In Flanders fields the poppies blow
Between the crosses, row on row,
That mark our place; and in the sky
The larks, still bravely singing, fly
Scarce heard amid the guns below.

We are the Dead. Short days ago
We lived, felt dawn, saw sunset glow,
Loved, and were loved, and now we lie
   In Flanders fields.

Take up our quarrel with the foe:
To you from failing hands we throw
The torch; be yours to hold it high.
If ye break faith with us who die
We shall not sleep, though poppies grow
   In Flanders fields.

WALTER DE LA MARE 1873–1956
THE LISTENERS

'Is there anybody there?' said the Traveller,
    Knocking on the moonlit door;
And his horse in the silence champed the grasses
    Of the forest's ferny floor:
And a bird flew up out of the turret,
    Above the Traveller's head:
And he smote upon the door again a second time;
    'Is there anybody there?' he said.
But no one descended to the Traveller;
    No head from the leaf-fringed sill
Leaned over and looked into his grey eyes,
    Where he stood perplexed and still.
But only a host of phantom listeners
    That dwelt in the lone house then
Stood listening in the quiet of the moonlight
    To that voice from the world of men:
Stood thronging the faint moonbeams on the dark stair,
    That goes down to the empty hall,
Harkening in an air stirred and shaken
    By the lonely Traveller's call.
And he felt in his heart their strangeness,
    Their stillness answering his cry,
While his horse moved, cropping the dark turf,
    'Neath the starred and leafy sky;
For he suddenly smote on the door, even
    Louder, and lifted his head: —
'Tell them I came, and no one answered,
    That I kept my word,' he said.
Never the least stir made the listeners,
    Though every word he spake

Fell echoing through the shadowiness of the still house
    From the one man left awake:
Ay, they heard his foot upon the stirrup,
    And the sound of iron on stone,
And how the silence surged softly backward,
When the plunging hoofs were gone.

DYLAN THOMAS 1914—53

FERN HILL

Now as I was young and easy under the apple boughs
About the lilting house and happy as the grass was green,
   The night above the dingle starry,
      Time let me hail and climb
   Golden in the heydays of his eyes,
And honoured among wagons I was prince of the apple towns
And once below a time I lordly had the trees and leaves
      Trail with daisies and barley
   Down the rivers of the windfall light.

And as I was green and carefree, famous among the barns
About the happy yard and singing as the farm was home,
   In the sun that is young once only,
      Time let me play and be
   Golden in the mercy of his means,
And green and golden I was huntsman and herdsman, the calves
Sang to my horn, the foxes on the hills barked clear and cold,
      And the sabbath rang slowly
   In the pebbles of the holy streams.

All the sun long it was running, it was lovely, the hay
Fields high as the house, the tunes from the chimneys, it was air
   And playing, lovely and watery
      And fire green as grass.
   And nightly under the simple stars
As I rode to sleep the owls were bearing the farm away,
All the moon long I heard, blessed among stables, the night-jars
   Flying with the ricks, and the horses
      Flashing into the dark.

And then to awake, and the farm, like a wanderer white
With the dew, come back, the cock on his shoulder: it was all
    Shining, it was Adam and maiden,
        The sky gathered again
    And the sun grew round that very day,
So it must have been after the birth of the simple light
In the first, spinning place, the spellbound horses walking warm
    Out of the whinnying green stable
        On to the fields of praise.

And honoured among foxes and pheasants by the gay house
Under the new made clouds and happy as the heart was long,
    In the sun born over and over,
        I ran my heedless ways,
    My wishes raced through the house high hay
And nothing I cared, at my sky blue trades, that time allows
In all his tuneful turning so few and such morning songs
    Before the children green and golden
        Follow him out of grace.

Nothing I cared, in the lamb white days, that time would take me
Up to the swallow thronged loft by the shadow of my hand,
    In the moon that is always rising,
        Nor that riding to sleep
    I should hear him fly with the high fields
And wake to the farm forever fled from the childless land.
Oh as I was young and easy in the mercy of his means,
        Time held me green and dying
    Though I sang in my chains like the sea.

ALFRED, LORD TENNYSON 1809–92

THE CHARGE OF THE LIGHT BRIGADE

I

Half a league, half a league,
  Half a league onward,
All in the valley of Death
  Rode the six hundred.
'Forward, the Light Brigade!
Charge for the guns!' he said;
Into the valley of Death
  Rode the six hundred.

II

'Forward, the Light Brigade!'
Was there a man dismay'd?
Not tho' the soldier knew
  Some one had blunder'd:
Theirs not to make reply,
Theirs not to reason why,
Theirs but to do and die:
Into the valley of Death
  Rode the six hundred.

III

Cannon to right of them,
Cannon to left of them,
Cannon in front of them
  Volley'd and thunder'd;
Storm'd at with shot and shell,
Boldly they rode and well,
Into the jaws of Death,
Into the mouth of Hell
  Rode the six hundred.

IV

Flash'd all their sabres bare,
Flash'd as they turn'd in air,
Sabring the gunners there,
Charging an army, while
    All the world wonder'd:
Plunged in the battery-smoke
Right thro' the line they broke;
Cossack and Russian
Reel'd from the sabre-stroke
    Shatter'd and sunder'd.
Then they rode back, but not,
    Not the six hundred.

V

Cannon to right of them,
Cannon to left of them,
Cannon behind them
    Volley'd and thunder'd;
Storm'd at with shot and shell,
While horse and hero fell,
They that had fought so well
Came thro' the jaws of Death
Back from the mouth of Hell,
All that was left of them,
    Left of six hundred.

VI

When can their glory fade?
O the wild charge they made!
    All the world wonder'd.
Honour the charge they made!
Honour the Light Brigade,
    Noble six hundred!

E. E. CUMMINGS 1894–1962

I CARRY YOUR HEART WITH ME(I CARRY IT IN

i carry your heart with me(i carry it in
my heart)i am never without it(anywhere
i go you go,my dear;and whatever is done
by only me is your doing,my darling)
                                    i fear
no fate(for you are my fate,my sweet)i want
no world(for beautiful you are my world,my true)
and it's you are whatever a moon has always meant
and whatever a sun will always sing is you

here is the deepest secret nobody knows
(here is the root of the root and the bud of the bud
and the sky of the sky of a tree called life;which grows
higher than soul can hope or mind can hide)
and this is the wonder that's keeping the stars apart

i carry your heart(i carry it in my heart)

HILAIRE BELLOC 1870–1953

TARANTELLA

Do you remember an Inn,
Miranda?
Do you remember an Inn?
And the tedding and the spreading
Of the straw for a bedding,
And the fleas that tease in the High Pyrenees,
And the wine that tasted of the tar?
And the cheers and the jeers of the young muleteers
(Under the dark of the vine verandah)?
Do you remember an Inn, Miranda,
Do you remember an Inn?
And the cheers and the jeers of the young muleteers
Who hadn't got a penny,
And who weren't paying any,
And the hammer at the doors and the din?
And the hip! hop! hap!
Of the clap
Of the hands to the twirl and the swirl
Of the girl gone chancing,
Glancing,
Dancing,
Backing and advancing,
Snapping of the clapper to the spin
Out and in –
And the ting, tong, tang of the guitar!
Do you remember an Inn,
Miranda?
Do you remember an Inn?

Never more;
Miranda,
Never more.
Only the high peaks hoar;
And Aragon a torrent at the door.
No sound
In the walls of the halls where falls
The tread
Of the feet of the dead to the ground,
No sound:
Only the boom
Of the far waterfall like doom.

WILLIAM HENRY DAVIES 1871–1940

LEISURE

What is this life if, full of care,
We have no time to stand and stare.

No time to stand beneath the boughs
And stare as long as sheep or cows.

No time to see, when woods we pass,
Where squirrels hide their nuts in grass.

No time to see, in broad daylight,
Streams full of stars, like skies at night.

No time to turn at Beauty's glance,
And watch her feet, how they can dance.

No time to wait till her mouth can
Enrich that smile her eyes began.

A poor life this if, full of care,
We have no time to stand and stare.

JOHN MASEFIELD 1878–1967
CARGOES

Quinquireme of Nineveh from distant Ophir
Rowing home to haven in sunny Palestine,
With a cargo of ivory,
And apes and peacocks,
Sandalwood, cedarwood, and sweet white wine.

Stately Spanish galleon coming from the Isthmus,
Dipping through the Tropics by the palm-green shores,
With a cargo of diamonds,
Emeralds, amethysts,
Topazes, and cinnamon and gold moidores.

Dirty British coaster with a salt-caked smoke stack
Butting through the Channel in the mad March days,
With a cargo of Tyne coal,
Road-rail, pig-lead,
Firewood, iron-ware, and cheap tin trays.

JOHN MASEFIELD 1878–1967

SEA-FEVER

I must go down to the seas again, to the lonely sea and the sky,
And all I ask is a tall ship and a star to steer her by,
And the wheel's kick and the wind's song and the white sail's shaking,
And a grey mist on the sea's face and a grey dawn breaking.

I must go down to the seas again, for the call of the running tide
Is a wild call and a clear call that may not be denied;
And all I ask is a windy day with the white clouds flying,
And the flung spray and the blown spume, and the sea-gulls crying.

I must go down to the seas again, to the vagrant gypsy life,
To the gull's way and the whale's way where the wind's like a whetted knife;
And all I ask is a merry yarn from a laughing fellow-rover,
And quiet sleep and a sweet dream when the long trick's over.

SAMUEL TAYLOR COLERIDGE 1772–1834

KUBLA KHAN

In Xanadu did Kubla Khan
A stately pleasure-dome decree:
Where Alph, the sacred river, ran
Through caverns measureless to man
    Down to a sunless sea.
So twice five miles of fertile ground
With walls and towers were girdled round:
And here were gardens bright with sinuous rills,
Where blossomed many an incense-bearing tree;
And here were forests ancient as the hills
Enfolding sunny spots of greenery.

But oh! that deep romantic chasm which slanted
Down the green hill athwart a cedarn cover!
A savage place! as holy and enchanted
As e'er beneath a waning moon was haunted
By woman wailing for her demon-lover!
And from this chasm, with ceaseless turmoil seething,
As if this earth in fast thick pants were breathing,
A mighty fountain momently was forced:
Amid whose swift half-intermitted burst
Huge fragments vaulted like rebounding hail,
Or chaffy grain beneath the thresher's flail;
And 'mid these dancing rocks at once and ever
It flung up momently the sacred river.
Five miles meandering with a mazy motion
Through wood and dale the sacred river ran,
Then reached the caverns measureless to man,
And sank in tumult to a lifeless ocean:
And 'mid this tumult Kubla heard from far
Ancestral voices prophesying war!

The shadow of the dome of pleasure
Floated midway on the waves;
Where was heard the mingled measure
From the fountain and the caves.
It was a miracle of rare device,
A sunny pleasure-dome with caves of ice!

A damsel with a dulcimer
In a vision once I saw:
It was an Abyssinian maid,
And on her dulcimer she played,
Singing of Mount Abora.
Could I revive within me
Her symphony and song,
To such a deep delight 'twould win me,
That with music loud and long,
I would build that dome in air,
That sunny dome! those caves of ice!
And all who heard should see them there,
And all should cry, Beware! Beware!
His flashing eyes, his floating hair!
Weave a circle round him thrice,
And close your eyes with holy dread,
For he on honey-dew hath fed,
And drunk the milk of Paradise.

RUTH DALLAS 1919–

MILKING BEFORE DAWN

In the drifting rain the cows in the yard are as black
And wet and shiny as rocks in an ebbing tide;
But they smell of the soil, as leaves lying under trees
Smell of the soil, damp and steaming, warm.
The shed is an island of light and warmth, the night
Was water-cold and starless out in the paddock.

Crouched on the stool, hearing only the beat
The monotonous beat and hiss of the smooth machines,
The choking gasp of the cups and rattle of hooves,
How easy to fall asleep again, to think
Of the man in the city asleep; he does not feel
The night encircle him, the grasp of mud.

But now the hills in the east return, are soft
And grey with mist, the night recedes, and the rain.
The earth as it turns towards the sun is young
Again, renewed, its history wiped away
Like the tears of a child. Can the earth be young again
And not the heart? Let the man in the city sleep.

SONNET 116

Let me not to the marriage of true minds
Admit impediments. Love is not love
Which alters when it alteration finds,
Or bends with the remover to remove:
O no, it is an ever-fixed mark,
That looks on tempests and is never shaken;
It is the star to every wand'ring bark,
Whose worth's unknown although his height be taken.
Love's not Time's fool, though rosy lips and cheeks
Within his bending sickle's compass come;
Love alters not with his brief hours and weeks,
But bears it out even to the edge of doom.
    If this be error and upon me proved,
    I never writ, nor no man ever loved.

ROBERT FROST 1874–1963

STOPPING BY WOODS ON
A SNOWY EVENING

Whose woods these are I think I know.
His house is in the village though;
He will not see me stopping here
To watch his woods fill up with snow.

My little horse must think it queer
To stop without a farmhouse near
Between the woods and frozen lake
The darkest evening of the year.

He gives his harness bells a shake
To ask if there is some mistake.
The only other sound's the sweep
Of easy wind and downy flake.

The woods are lovely, dark and deep.
But I have promises to keep,
And miles to go before I sleep,
And miles to go before I sleep.

GERARD MANLEY HOPKINS 1844–89

THE WINDHOVER

To Christ our Lord

I caught this morning morning's minion kingdom
  of daylight's dauphin, dapple-dawn-drawn Falcon, in his riding
  Of the rolling level underneath him steady air, and striding
High there, how he rung upon the rein of a wimpling wing
In his ecstasy! then off, off forth on swing,
  As a skate's heel sweeps smooth on a bow-bend: the hurl and gliding
  Rebuffed the big wind. My heart in hiding
Stirred for a bird, – the achieve of, the mastery of the thing!

Brute beauty and valour and act, oh, air, pride, plume, here
  Buckle! AND the fire that breaks from thee then, a billion
Times told lovelier, more dangerous, O my chevalier!

  No wonder of it: sheer plod makes plough down sillion
Shine, and blue-bleak embers, ah my dear,
  Fall, gall themselves, and gash gold vermilion.

L.E. SCOTT 1947–

THROUGHOUT LIFE

As I go through life

I will at least make six friendships

So when I die

I will not have to walk to my grave

With six strangers complaining about

The heavy load

MAYA ANGELOU 1928–

PHENOMENAL WOMAN

Pretty women wonder where my secret lies.
I'm not cute or built to suit a fashion model's size
But when I start to tell them,
They think I'm telling lies.
I say,
It's in the reach of my arms
The span of my hips,
The stride of my step,
The curl of my lips.
I'm a woman
Phenomenally.
Phenomenal woman,
That's me.

I walk into a room
Just as cool as you please,
And to a man,
The fellows stand or
Fall down on their knees.
Then they swarm around me,
A hive of honey bees.
I say,
It's the fire in my eyes,
And the flash of my teeth,
The swing in my waist,
And the joy in my feet.
I'm a woman
Phenomenally.
Phenomenal woman,
That's me.

Men themselves have wondered
What they see in me.
They try so much
But they can't touch
My inner mystery.
When I try to show them
They say they still can't see.
I say,
It's in the arch of my back,
The sun of my smile,
The ride of my breasts,
The grace of my style.
I'm a woman
Phenomenally.
Phenomenal woman,
That's me.

Now you understand
Just why my head's not bowed.
I don't shout or jump about
Or have to talk real loud.
When you see me passing
It ought to make you proud.
I say,
It's in the click of my heels,
The bend of my hair,
The palm of my hand,
The need of my care,
'Cause I'm a woman
Phenomenally.
Phenomenal woman,
That's me.

A.B. 'BANJO' PATERSON 1864–1941

THE MAN FROM SNOWY RIVER

There was movement at the station, for the word had passed around
That the colt from old Regret had got away,
And had joined the wild bush horses – he was worth a thousand pound,
So all the cracks had gathered to the fray.
All the tried and noted riders from the stations near and far
Had mustered at the homestead overnight,
For the bushmen love hard riding where the wild bush horses are,
And the stock-horse snuffs the battle with delight.

There was Harrison, who made his pile when Pardon won the cup,
The old man with his hair as white as snow;
But few could ride beside him when his blood was fairly up –
He would go wherever horse and man could go.
And Clancy of the Overflow came down to lend a hand,
No better horseman ever held the reins;
For never horse could throw him while the saddle-girths would stand,
He learnt to ride while droving on the plains.

And one was there, a stripling on a small and weedy beast,
He was something like a racehorse undersized,
With a touch of Timor pony – three parts thoroughbred at least –
And such as are by mountain horsemen prized.
He was hard and tough and wiry – just the sort that won't say die –
There was courage in his quick impatient tread;
And he bore the badge of gameness in his bright and fiery eye,
And the proud and lofty carriage of his head.

But still so slight and weedy, one would doubt his power to stay,
And the old man said, 'That horse will never do
For a long and tiring gallop – lad, you'd better stop away,
Those hills are far too rough for such as you.'

So he waited, sad and wistful — only Clancy stood his friend —
'I think we ought to let him come,' he said;
'I warrant he'll be with us when he's wanted at the end,
For both his horse and he are mountain bred.'

'He hails from Snowy River, up by Kosciusko's side,
Where the hills are twice as steep and twice as rough;
Where a horse's hoofs strike firelight from the flint stones every stride,
That man that holds his own is good enough.
And the Snowy River riders on the mountains make their home,
Where the river runs those giant hills between;
I have seen full many horsemen since I first commenced to roam,
But nowhere yet such horsemen have I seen.'

So he went, they found the horses by the big mimosa clump,
They raced away towards the mountain's brow,
And the old man gave his orders, 'Boys, go at them from the jump,
No use to try for fancy riding now.
And, Clancy, you must wheel them, try and wheel them to the right.
Ride boldly, lad, and never fear the spills,
For never yet was rider that could keep the mob in sight,
If once they gain the shelter of those hills.'

So Clancy rode to wheel them — he was racing on the wing
Where the best and boldest riders take their place,
And he raced his stock-horse past them, and he made the ranges ring
With the stockwhip, as he met them face to face.
Then they halted for a moment, while he swung the dreaded lash,
But they saw their well-loved mountain full in view,
And they charged beneath the stockwhip with a sharp and sudden dash,
And off into the mountain scrub they flew.

Then fast the horsemen followed, where the gorges deep and black
Resounded to the thunder of their tread,
And the stockwhips woke the echoes, and they fiercely answered back

From cliffs and crags that beetled overhead.
And upward, ever upward, the wild horses held their way,
Where mountain ash and kurrajong grew wide;
And the old man muttered fiercely, 'We may bid the mob good day,
No man can hold them down the other side.'

When they reached the mountain's summit, even Clancy took a pull –
It well might make the boldest hold their breath;
The wild hop scrub grew thickly, and the hidden ground was full
Of wombat holes, and any slip was death.
But the man from Snowy River let the pony have his head,
And he swung his stockwhip round and gave a cheer,
And he raced him down the mountain like a torrent down its bed,
While the others stood and watched in very fear.

He sent the flint stones flying, but the pony kept his feet,
He cleared the fallen timber in his stride,
And the man from Snowy River never shifted in his seat –
It was grand to see that mountain horseman ride.
Through the stringy barks and saplings, on the rough and broken ground,
Down the hillside at a racing pace he went;
And he never drew the bridle till he landed safe and sound,
At the bottom of that terrible descent.

He was right among the horses as they climbed the farther hill,
And the watchers on the mountain standing mute,
Saw him ply the stockwhip fiercely, he was right among them still,
As he raced across the clearing in pursuit.
Then they lost him for a moment, where two mountain gullies met
In the ranges, but a final glimpse reveals
On a dim and distant hillside the wild horses racing yet,
With the man from Snowy River at their heels.

And he ran them single-handed till their sides were white with foam.
He followed like a bloodhound on their track,
Till they halted, cowed and beaten; then he turned their heads for home,

And alone and unassisted brought them back.
But his hardy mountain pony he could scarcely raise a trot,
He was blood from hip to shoulder from the spur;
But his pluck was still undaunted, and his courage fiery hot,
For never yet was mountain horse a cur.

And down by Kosciusko, where the pine-clad ridges raise
Their torn and rugged battlements on high,
Where the air is clear as crystal, and the white stars fairly blaze
At midnight in the cold and frosty sky,
And where around the Overflow the reedbeds sweep and sway
To the breezes, and the rolling plains are wide,
The man from Snowy River is a household word today,
And the stockmen tell the story of his ride.

GERARD MANLEY HOPKINS 1844–89

PIED BEAUTY

Glory be to God for dappled things –
   For skies of couple-colour as a brinded cow;
     For rose-moles all in stipple upon trout that swim;
Fresh-firecoal chestnut-falls; finches' wings;
   Landscape plotted and pieced – fold, fallow, and plough;
     And all trades, their gear and tackle and trim.

All things counter, original, spare, strange;
   Whatever is fickle, freckled (who knows how?)
     With swift, slow; sweet, sour; adazzle, dim;
He fathers-forth whose beauty is past change:
        Praise him.

THE RAVEN

Once upon a midnight dreary, while I pondered, weak and weary,
Over many a quaint and curious volume of forgotten lore –
While I nodded, nearly napping, suddenly there came a tapping,
As of some one gently rapping – rapping at my chamber door
''Tis some visitor,' I muttered, 'tapping at my chamber door –
      Only this and nothing more.'

Ah, distinctly I remember, it was in the bleak December,
And each separate dying ember wrought its ghost upon the floor.
Eagerly I wished the morrow; – vainly I had sought to borrow
From my books surcease of sorrow – sorrow for the lost Lenore –
For the rare and radiant maiden whom the angels name Lenore –
      Nameless here for evermore.

And the silken sad uncertain rustling of each purple curtain
Thrilled me – filled me with fantastic terrors never felt before;
So that now, to still the beating of my heart, I stood repeating
''Tis some visitor entreating entrance at my chamber door –
Some late visitor entreating entrance at my chamber door; –
      This it is and nothing more.'

Presently my soul grew stronger; hesitating then no longer,
'Sir,' said I, 'or, Madam, truly your forgiveness I implore;
But the fact is I was napping, and so gently you came rapping,
And so faintly you came tapping – tapping at my chamber door,
That I scarce was sure I heard you' – here I opened wide the door:–
      Darkness there and nothing more.

Deep into that darkness peering, long I stood there wondering, fearing,
Doubting, dreaming dreams no mortal ever dared to dream before;
But the silence was unbroken, and the darkness gave no token,
And the only word there spoken was the whispered word, 'Lenore!' –
This I whispered, and an echo murmured back the word, 'Lenore!'
      Merely this and nothing more.

Then into the chamber turning, all my soul within me burning.
Soon again I heard a tapping somewhat louder than before.
'Surely,' said I, 'surely that is something at my window lattice;
Let me see, then, what thereat is, and this mystery explore –
Let my heart be still a moment, and this mystery explore; –
      'Tis the wind and nothing more.'

Open here I flung the shutter, when, with many a flirt and flutter,
In there stepped a stately Raven of the saintly days of yore.
Not the least obeisance made he; not an instant stopped or stayed he;
But, with mien of lord or lady, perched above my chamber door –
Perched upon a bust of Pallas just above my chamber door –
      Perched, and sat, and nothing more.

Then this ebony bird beguiling my sad fancy into smiling,
By the grave and stern decorum of the countenance it wore,
'Though thy crest be shorn and shaven, thou,' I said, 'art sure no craven,
Ghastly grim and ancient Raven wandering from the Nightly shore –
Tell me what thy Lordly name is on the Night's Plutonian shore!'
      Quoth the Raven, 'Nevermore.'

Much I marvelled this ungainly fowl to hear discourse so plainly,
Though its answer little meaning – little relevancy bore;
For we cannot help agreeing that no living human being
Ever yet was blessed with seeing bird above his chamber door,
Ever yet was blessed with seeing bird above his chamber door –
      With such name as 'Nevermore.'

But the Raven, sitting lonely on that placid bust, spoke only
That one word, as if his soul in that one word he did out-pour.
Nothing further then he uttered; not a feather then he fluttered –
Till I scarcely more than muttered, 'Other friends have flown before –
On the morrow *he* will leave me, as my Hopes have flown before.'
      Then the bird said, 'Nevermore.'

Startled at the stillness broken by reply so aptly spoken,
'Doubtless,' said I, 'what it utters is its only stock and store,
Caught from some unhappy master, whom unmerciful Disaster

Followed fast and followed faster till his songs one burden bore —
Till the dirges of his Hope the melancholy burden bore
       Of 'Never — nevermore.'

But the Raven still beguiling all my sad soul into smiling,
Straight I wheeled a cushioned seat in front of bird and bust and door;
Then, upon the velvet sinking, I betook myself to linking
Fancy unto fancy, thinking what this ominous bird of yore —
What this grim, ungainly, ghastly, gaunt, and ominous bird of yore
       Meant in croaking 'Nevermore.'

This I sat engaged in guessing, but no syllable expressing
To the fowl whose fiery eyes now burned into my bosom's core;
This and more I sat divining, with my head at ease reclining
On the cushion's velvet violet lining that the lamp-light gloated o'er,
But whose velvet violet lining with the lamp-light gloating o'er,
       She shall press, ah, nevermore!

Then, methought, the air grew denser, perfumed from an unseen censer
Swung by Seraphim whose foot-falls tinkled on the tufted floor.
'Wretch,' I cried, 'thy God hath lent thee — by these angels he hath sent thee
Respite — respite and nepenthe from thy memories of Lenore!
Quaff, oh quaff this kind nepenthe, and forget this lost Lenore!'
       Quoth the Raven, 'Nevermore.'

'Prophet!' said I, 'thing of evil! — prophet still, if bird or devil! —
Whether Tempter sent or whether tempest tossed thee here ashore,
Desolate yet all undaunted, on this desert land enchanted —
On this home by Horror haunted — tell me truly, I implore —
Is there — *is* there balm in Gilead? — tell me — tell me, I implore!'
       Quoth the Raven, 'Nevermore.'

'Prophet!' said I, 'thing of evil — prophet still, if bird or devil!
By that Heaven that bends above us — by that God we both adore —
Tell this soul with sorrow laden if, within the distant Aidenn,
It shall clasp a sainted maiden whom the angels name Lenore —
Clasp a rare and radiant maiden whom the angels name Lenore.'
       Quoth the Raven, 'Nevermore.'

'Be that word our sign of parting, bird or fiend!' I shrieked, upstarting –
'Get thee back into the tempest and the Night's Plutonian shore!
Leave no black plume as a token of that lie thy soul hath spoken!
Leave my loneliness unbroken! – quit the bust above my door!
Take thy beak from out my heart, and take thy form from off my door!'
        Quoth the Raven, 'Nevermore.'

And the Raven, never flitting, still is sitting – still is sitting
On the pallid bust of Pallas just above my chamber door;
And his eyes have all the seeming of a Demon's that is dreaming,
And the lamp-light o'er him streaming throws his shadow on the floor;
And my soul from out that shadow that lies floating on the floor
        Shall be lifted – nevermore!

WILLIAM WORDSWORTH 1770–1850

UPON WESTMINSTER BRIDGE

Sept. 3, 1802

Earth has not anything to show more fair:
Dull would he be of soul who could pass by
A sight so touching in its majesty:
This City now doth like a garment wear

The beauty of the morning: silent, bare,
Ships, towers, domes, theatres, and temples lie
Open unto the fields, and to the sky,
All bright and glittering in the smokeless air.

Never did sun more beautifully steep
In his first splendour valley, rock, or hill;
Ne'er saw I, never felt, a calm so deep!

The river glideth at his own sweet will:
Dear God! the very houses seem asleep;
And all that mighty heart is lying still!

WILFRED OWEN 1893–1918

DULCE ET DECORUM EST

Bent double, like old beggars under sacks,
Knocked-kneed, coughing like hags, we cursed through sludge,
Till on the haunting flares we turned our backs
And towards our distant rest began to trudge.
Men marched asleep. Many had lost their boots
But limped on, blood-shod. All went lame; all blind;
Drunk with fatigue; deaf even to the hoots
Of tired, outstripped Five-Nines that dropped behind.

Gas! Gas! Quick, boys! – An ecstasy of fumbling,
Fitting the clumsy helmets just in time;
But someone still was yelling out and stumbling
And flound'ring like a man in fire or lime...
Dim, through the misty panes and thick green light,
As under a green sea, I saw him drowning.

In all my dreams, before my helpless sight,
He plunges at me, guttering, choking, drowning.

If in some smothering dreams you too could pace
Behind the wagon that we flung him in,
And watch the white eyes writhing in his face,
His hanging face, like a devil's sick of sin;
If you could hear, at every jolt, the blood
Come gargling from the froth-corrupted lungs,
Obscene as cancer, bitter as the cud
Of vile, incurable sores on innocent tongues, –
My friend, you would not tell with such high zest
To children ardent for some desperate glory,
The old Lie: Dulce et Decorum est
Pro patria mori.

ELIZABETH BARRETT BROWNING 1806–61

From SONNETS FROM THE PORTUGUESE

XLIII

How do I love thee? Let me count the ways.
I love thee to the depth and breadth and height
My soul can reach, when feeling out of sight
For the ends of Being and ideal Grace.
I love thee to the level of everyday's
Most quiet need, by sun and candlelight.
I love thee freely, as men strive for Right;
I love thee purely, as they turn from Praise.
I love thee with the passion put to use
In my old griefs, and with my childhood's faith.
I love thee with a love I seemed to lose
With my lost saints, – I love thee with the breath,
Smiles, tears, of all my life! – and, if God choose,
I shall but love thee better after death.

THOMAS GRAY 1716–71

ELEGY WRITTEN IN A
COUNTRY CHURCHYARD

The curfew tolls the knell of parting day,
  The lowing herd wind slowly o'er the lea,
The plowman homeward plods his weary way,
  And leaves the world to darkness and to me.

Now fades the glimmering landscape on the sight,
  And all the air a solemn stillness holds,
Save where the beetle wheels his droning flight,
  And drowsy tinklings lull the distant folds.

Save that from yonder ivy-mantled tower
  The moping owl does to the moon complain
Of such as, wandering near her secret bower,
  Molest her ancient solitary reign.

Beneath those rugged elms, that yew-tree's shade,
  Where heaves the turf in many a mouldering heap,
Each in his narrow cell for ever laid,
  The rude forefathers of the hamlet sleep.

The breezy call of incense-breathing morn,
  The swallow twittering from the straw-built shed,
The cock's shrill clarion, or the echoing horn,
  No more shall rouse them from their lowly bed.

For them no more the blazing hearth shall burn,
  Or busy housewife ply her evening care:
No children run to lisp their sire's return,
  Or climb his knee the envied kiss to share.

Oft did the harvest to their sickle yield,
  Their furrow of the stubborn glebe has broke:
How jocund did they drive their team afield!
  How bowed the woods beneath their sturdy stroke!

Let not ambition mock their useful toil,
   Their homely joys, and destiny obscure;
Nor grandeur hear with a disdainful smile
   The short and simple annals of the poor.

The boast of heraldry, the pomp of power,
   And all that beauty, all that wealth e'er gave,
Awaits alike the inevitable hour.
   The paths of glory lead but to the grave.

Nor you, ye proud, impute to these the fault,
   If memory o'er their tomb no trophies raise,
Where through the long-drawn aisle and fretted vault
   The pealing anthem swells the note of praise.

Can storied urn or animated bust
   Back to its mansion call the fleeting breath?
Can honour's voice provoke the silent dust,
   Or flattery soothe the dull cold ear of death?

Perhaps in this neglected spot is laid
   Some heart once pregnant with celestial fire;
Hands, that the rod of empire might have swayed,
Or waked to ecstasy the living lyre.

But knowledge to their eyes her ample page
   Rich with the spoils of time did ne'er unroll;
Chill penury repressed their noble rage,
   And froze the genial current of the soul.

Full many a gem of purest ray serene,
   The dark unfathomed caves of ocean bear;
Full many a flower is born to blush unseen,
   And waste its sweetness on the desert air.

Some village-Hampden, that with dauntless breast
   The little tyrant of his fields withstood,
Some mute inglorious Milton here may rest,
   Some Cromwell guiltless of his country's blood.

The applause of listening senates to command.
    The threats of pain and ruin to despise,
To scatter plenty o'er a smiling land,
    And read their history in a nation's eyes,

Their lot forbad: nor circumscribed alone
    Their growing virtues, but their crimes confined;
Forbad to wade through slaughter to a throne,
And shut the gates of mercy on mankind,

The struggling pangs of conscious truth to hide,
    To quench the blushes of ingenuous shame,
Or heap the shrine of luxury and pride
    With incense kindled at the Muse's flame.

Far from the madding crowd's ignoble strife,
    Their sober wishes never learned to stray;
Along the cool sequestered vale of life
    They kept the noiseless tenor of their way.

Yet even those bones from insult to protect
    Some frail memorial still erected nigh,
With uncouth rhymes and shapeless sculpture decked,
    Implores the passing tribute of a sigh.

Their name, their years, spelt by the unlettered Muse,
    The place of fame and elegy supply:
And many a holy text around she strews,
    That teach the rustic moralist to die.

For who, to dumb forgetfulness a prey,
    This pleasing anxious being e'er resigned,
Left the warm precincts of the cheerful day,
    Nor cast one longing lingering look behind?

On some fond breast the parting soul relies,
    Some pious drops the closing eye requires;
E'en from the tomb the voice of nature cries,
    E'en in our ashes live their wonted fires.

For thee, who mindful of the unhonoured dead,
    Dost in these lines their artless tale relate;
If chance, by lonely contemplation led,
    Some kindred spirit shall inquire thy fate –

Haply some hoary-headed swain may say,
    'Oft have we seen him at the peep of dawn
Brushing with hasty steps the dews away
    To meet the sun upon the upland lawn.

'There at the foot of yonder nodding beech,
    That wreathes its old fantastic roots so high,
His listless length at noontide would he stretch,
    And pore upon the brook that babbles by.

'Hard by yon wood, now smiling as in scorn,
    Muttering his wayward fancies he would rove,
Now drooping, woeful-wan, like one forlorn,
    Or crazed with care, or crossed in hopeless love.

'One morn I missed him on the customed hill,
    Along the heath, and near his favourite tree;
Another came; nor yet beside the rill,
    Nor up the lawn, nor at the wood was he:

'The next, with dirges due in sad array
    Slow through the church-way path we saw him borne.
Approach and read (for thou can'st read) the lay,
    Graved on the stone beneath yon aged thorn.'

(There scattered oft, the earliest of the year,
    By hands unseen, are showers of violets found:
The redbreast loves to bill and warble there,
    And little footsteps lightly print the ground.)

THE EPITAPH

Here rests his head upon the lap of Earth
A Youth, to Fortune and to Fame unknown.
Fair Science frowned not on his humble birth,
And Melancholy marked him for her own.

Large was his bounty, and his soul sincere,
Heaven did a recompense as largely send;
He gave to Misery all he had, a tear,
He gained from Heaven ('twas all he wished) a friend.

No farther seek his merits to disclose,
Or draw his frailties from their dread abode,
(There they alike in trembling hope repose,)
The bosom of his Father and his God.

JAMES K. BAXTER 1926–72

THE MAORI JESUS

I saw the Maori Jesus
Walking on Wellington Harbour.
He wore blue dungarees.
His beard and hair were long.
His breath smelt of mussels and paraoa.
When he smiled it looked like the dawn.
When he broke wind the little fishes trembled.
When he frowned the ground shook.
When he laughed everybody got drunk.

The Maori Jesus came on shore
And picked out his twelve disciples.
One cleaned toilets in the Railway Station;
His hands were scrubbed red to get the shit out of
        the pores.
One was a call-girl who turned it up for nothing.
One was a housewife who'd forgotten the Pill
And stuck her TV set in the rubbish can.
One was a little office clerk
Who'd tried to set fire to the Government Buildings.
Yes, and there were several others;
One was an old sad quean;
One was an alcoholic priest
Going slowly mad in a respectable parish.

The Maori Jesus said, 'Man,
From now on the sun will shine.'

He did no miracles;
He played the guitar sitting on the ground.

The first day he was arrested
For having no lawful means of support.
The second day he was beaten up by the cops
For telling a dee his house was not in order.
The third day he was charged with being a Maori
And given a month in Mount Crawford.
The fourth day he was sent to Porirua
For telling a screw the sun would stop rising.
The fifth day lasted seven years
While he worked in the asylum laundry
Never out of the steam.
The sixth day he told the head doctor,
'I am the Light in the Void;
I am who I am.'
The seventh day he was lobotomized;
The brain of God was cut in half.

On the eighth day the sun did not rise.
It didn't rise the day after.
God was neither alive nor dead.
The darkness of the Void,
Mountainous, mile-deep, civilized darkness
Sat on the earth from then till now.

ODE TO A NIGHTINGALE

My heart aches, and a drowsy numbness pains
  My sense, as though of hemlock I had drunk,
Or emptied some dull opiate to the drains
  One minute past, and Lethe-wards had sunk:
'Tis not through envy of thy happy lot,
  But being too happy in thy happiness, –
    That thou, light-winged Dryad of the trees,
      In some melodious plot
  Of beechen green, and shadows numberless,
    Singest of summer in full-throated ease.

O for a draught of vintage! that hath been
  Cool'd a long age in the deep-delved earth,
Tasting of Flora and the country-green,
  Dance, and Provençal song, and sunburnt mirth.
O for a beaker full of the warm South,
  Full of the true, the blushful Hippocrene,
    With beaded bubbles winking at the brim
      And purple-stained mouth;
  That I might drink, and leave the world unseen,
    And with thee fade away into the forest dim.

Fade far away, dissolve, and quite forget
  What thou among the leaves hast never known,
The weariness, the fever, and the fret
  Here, where men sit and hear each other groan;
Where palsy shakes a few, sad, last grey hairs,
  Where youth grows pale, and spectre-thin, and dies;
    Where but to think is to be full of sorrow
      And leaden-eyed despairs;
  Where Beauty cannot keep her lustrous eyes,
    Or new Love pine at them beyond tomorrow.

Away! away! for I will fly to thee,
  Not charioted by Bacchus and his pards,
But on the viewless wings of Poesy,
  Though the dull brain perplexes and retards:
Already with thee! tender is the night,
  And haply the Queen-Moon is on her throne,
    Cluster'd around by all her starry Fays;
      But here there is no light,
  Save what from heaven is with the breezes blown
    Through verdurous glooms and winding mossy ways.

I cannot see what flowers are at my feet,
  Nor what soft incense hangs upon the boughs,
But, in embalmed darkness, guess each sweet
  Wherewith the seasonable month endows
The grass, the thicket, and the fruit-tree wild;
  White hawthorn, and the pastoral eglantine;
    Fast-fading violets cover'd up in leaves;
      And mid-May's eldest child,
  The coming musk-rose, full of dewy wine,
    The murmurous haunt of flies on summer eves.

Darkling I listen; and for many a time
  I have been half in love with easeful Death,
Call'd him soft names in many a mused rhyme,
  To take into the air my quiet breath;
Now more than ever seems it rich to die,
  To cease upon the midnight with no pain,
    While thou art pouring forth thy soul abroad
      In such an ecstasy!
  Still wouldst thou sing, and I have ears in vain —
    To thy high requiem become a sod.

Thou wast not born for death, immortal Bird!
  No hungry generations tread thee down;
The voice I hear this passing night was heard

In ancient days by emperor and clown:
Perhaps the selfsame song that found a path
   Through the sad heart of Ruth, when, sick for home,
    She stood in tears amid the alien corn;
     The same that oft-times hath
  Charm'd magic casements, opening on the foam
   Of perilous seas, in faery lands forlorn.

Forlorn! the very word is like a bell
  To toll me back from thee to my sole self!
Adieu! the fancy cannot cheat so well
  As she is famed to do, deceiving elf.
Adieu! adieu! thy plaintive anthem fades
  Past the near meadows, over the still stream,
   Up the hill-side; and now 'tis buried deep
    In the next valley-glades:
  Was it a vision, or a waking dream?
  Fled is that music: – do I wake or sleep?

HILAIRE BELLOC 1870–1953

MATILDA

Who Told Lies, and Was Burned to Death

Matilda told such Dreadful Lies,
It made one Gasp and Stretch one's Eyes;
Her Aunt, who, from her Earliest Youth,
Had kept a Strict Regard for Truth,
Attempted to Believe Matilda:
The effort very nearly killed her,
And would have done so, had not She
Discovered this Infirmity.
For once, towards the Close of Day,
Matilda, growing tired of play,
And finding she was left alone,
Went tiptoe to the Telephone
And summoned the Immediate Aid
Of London's Noble Fire-Brigade.
Within an hour the Gallant Band
Were pouring in on every hand,
From Putney, Hackney Downs, and Bow.
With Courage high and Hearts a-glow,
They galloped, roaring through the Town,
'Matilda's House is Burning Down!'
Inspired by British Cheers and Loud
Proceeding from the Frenzied Crowd,
They ran their ladders through a score
Of windows on the Ball Room Floor;
And took Peculiar Pains to Souse
The Pictures up and down the House,
Until Matilda's Aunt succeeded
In showing them they were not needed;
And even then she had to pay
To get the Men to go away!

It happened that a few Weeks later
Her Aunt was off to the Theatre
To see that Interesting Play
The Second Mrs. Tanqueray.
She had refused to take her Niece
To hear this Entertaining Piece:
A Deprivation Just and Wise
To Punish her for Telling Lies.
That Night a Fire *did* break out —
You should have heard Matilda Shout!
You should have heard her Scream and Bawl,
And throw the window up and call
To People passing in the Street —
(The rapidly increasing Heat
Encouraging her to obtain
Their confidence) — but all in vain!
For every time she shouted 'Fire!'
They only answered 'Little Liar!'
And therefore when her Aunt returned,
Matilda, and the House, were Burned.

WILFRED OWEN 1893–1918

ANTHEM FOR DOOMED YOUTH

What passing-bells for these who die as cattle?
   Only the monstrous anger of the guns.
   Only the stuttering rifles' rapid rattle
Can patter out their hasty orisons.
No mockeries now for them; no prayers nor bells,
   Nor any voice of mourning save the choirs, –
The shrill, demented choirs of wailing shells;
   And bugles calling for them from sad shires.

What candles may be held to speed them all?
   Not in the hands of boys, but in their eyes
Shall shine the holy glimmers of good-byes.
   The pallor of girls' brows shall be their pall;
Their flowers the tenderness of patient minds,
And each slow dusk a drawing down of blinds.

WILLIAM SHAKESPEARE 1564–1616
SONNET 18

Shall I compare thee to a summer's day?
Thou art more lovely and more temperate.
Rough winds do shake the darling buds of May,
And summer's lease hath all too short a date.
Sometime too hot the eye of heaven shines,
And often is his gold complexion dimmed,
And every fair from fair sometime declines,
By chance or nature's changing course untrimm'd:
But thy eternal summer shall not fade
Nor lose possession of that fair thou ow'st,
Nor shall death brag thou wandr'st in his shade,
When in eternal lines to time thou grow'st,
    So long as men can breathe or eyes can see
    So long lives this, and this gives life to thee.

THE MAN FROM IRONBARK

It was the man from Ironbark who struck the Sydney town,
He wandered over street and park, he wandered up and down,
He loitered here, he loitered there, till he was like to drop,
Until at last in sheer despair he sought a barber's shop.
''Ere! shave me beard and whiskers off, I'll be a man of mark,
I'll go and do the Sydney toff up home in Ironbark!'

The barber man was small and flash, as barbers mostly are,
He wore a strike-your-fancy sash, he smoked a huge cigar:
He was a humorist of note and keen on repartee,
He laid the odds and kept a 'tote', whatever that might be.
And when he saw our friend arrive, he whispered, 'Here's a lark!
Just watch me catch him all alive, this man from Ironbark!'

There were some gilded youths that sat along the barber's wall,
Their eyes were dull, their heads were flat, they had no brains at all;
To them the barber passed the wink, his dexter eyelid shut,
'I'll make this bloomin' yokel think his bloomin' throat is cut.'
And as he soaped and rubbed it in, he made a rude remark:
'I s'pose the flats is pretty green up there in Ironbark.'

A grunt was all reply he got; he shaved the bushman's chin,
Then made the water boiling hot and dipped the razor in.
He raised his hand, his brow grew black, he paused awhile to gloat,
Then slashed the red-hot razor-back across his victim's throat;
Upon the newly-shaven skin it made a livid mark –
No doubt it fairly took him in – that man from Ironbark.

He fetched a wild up-country yell might wake the dead to hear,
And though his throat, he knew full well, was cut from ear to ear,
He struggled gamely to his feet, and faced the murderous foe.
'You've done for me! you dog, I'm beat! one hit before I go!
I only wish I had a knife, you blessed murdering shark!
But you'll remember all your life the man from Ironbark.'

He lifted up his hairy paw, with one tremendous clout
He landed on the barber's jaw, and knocked the barber out.
He set to work with tooth and nail, he made the place a wreck;
He grabbed the nearest gilded youth, and tried to break his neck.
And all the while his throat he held to save his vital spark,
And 'Murder! Bloody Murder!' yelled the man from Ironbark.

A peeler man who heard the din came in to see the show;
He tried to run the bushman in, but he refused to go.
And when at last the barber spoke, and said ''Twas all in fun –
'Twas just a little harmless joke, a trifle overdone.'
'A joke!' he cried, 'By George, that's fine; a lively sort of lark;
I'd like to catch that murdering swine some night in Ironbark.'

And now while round the shearing-floor the listening shearers gape,
He tells the story o'er and o'er, and brags of his escape.
'Them barber chaps what keeps a tote, by George, I've had enough,
One tried to cut my bloomin' throat, but thank the Lord it's tough.'
And whether he's believed or no, there's one thing to remark,
That flowing beards are all the go way up in Ironbark.

BRIAN TURNER 1944–

LIKE LAMPLIGHT

One day when you are beside me
invite me to speak
of the secrets I never knew
I wanted to tell you, of the warmth
I never knew I owned
until you released it
by moving close as lamplight seems
to glass. Ask me

why I came to you
with the reverence of one
who sees a flower bloom
where none has bloomed before.
By saying what is
I will have said what was.

Sometimes when you are content
ask me what it is
that moves me to want to hold you so,
so often, and laugh when I tell
you the same old
indestructible thing.

One day when you are
where you feel no invitation to be
I will tell you
how you flower
like lamplight in me.

BILL MANHIRE 1946–
EREBUS VOICES

The Mountain

I am here beside my brother, Terror.
I am the place of human error.

I am beauty and cloud, and I am sorrow;
I am tears which you will weep tomorrow.

I am the sky and the exhausting gale.
I am the place of ice. I am the debris trail.

And I am still a hand, a fingertip, a ring.
I am what there is no forgetting.

I am the one with truly broken heart.
I watched them fall, and freeze, and break apart.

The Dead

We fell.

Yet we were loved and we are lifted.

We froze.

Yet we were loved and we are warm.

We broke apart.

Yet we are here and we are whole.

From THE BALLAD OF READING GAOL

He did not wear his scarlet coat,
　　For blood and wine are red,
And blood and wine were on his hands
　　When they found him with the dead,
The poor dead woman whom he loved,
　　And murdered in her bed.

He walked amongst the Trial Men
　　In a suit of shabby grey;
A cricket cap was on his head,
　　And his step seemed light and gay;
But I never saw a man who looked
　　So wistfully at the day.

I never saw a man who looked
　　With such a wistful eye
Upon that little tent of blue
　　Which prisoners call the sky,
And at every drifting cloud that went
　　With sails of silver by.

I walked, with other souls in pain,
　　Within another ring,
And was wondering if the man had done
　　A great or little thing,
When a voice behind me whispered low,
　　That fellow's got to swing.

****

Six weeks our guardsman walked the yard,
　　In the suit of shabby grey:
His cricket cap was on his head,
　　And his step seemed light and gay,

But I never saw a man who looked
     So wistfully at the day.

I never saw a man who looked
     With such a wistful eye
Upon that little tent of blue
     Which prisoners call the sky,
And at every wandering cloud that trailed
     Its ravelled fleeces by.

He did not wring his hands, as do
     Those witless men who dare
To try to rear the changeling Hope
     In the cave of black Despair:
He only looked upon the sun,
     And drank the morning air.

He did not wring his hands nor weep,
     Nor did he peak or pine,
But he drank the air as though it held
     Some healthful anodyne;
With open mouth he drank the sun
     As though it had been wine!

And I and all the souls in pain,
     Who tramped the other ring,
Forgot if we ourselves had done
     A great or little thing,
And watched with gaze of dull amaze
     The man who had to swing.

And strange it was to see him pass
     With a step so light and gay,
And strange it was to see him look
     So wistfully at the day,
And strange it was to think that he
     Had such a debt to pay.

****

For oak and elm have pleasant leaves
      That in the spring-time shoot:
But grim to see is the gallows-tree,
      With its adder-bitten root,
And, green or dry, a man must die
      Before it bears its fruit!

The loftiest place is that seat of grace
      For which all worldlings try:
But who would stand in hempen band
      Upon a scaffold high,
And through a murderer's collar take
      His last look at the sky?

It is sweet to dance to violins
      When Love and Life are fair:
To dance to flutes, to dance to lutes
      Is delicate and rare:
But it is not sweet with nimble feet
      To dance upon the air!

So with curious eyes and sick surmise
      We watched him day by day,
And wondered if each one of us
      Would end the self-same way,
For none can tell to what red Hell
      His sightless soul may stray.

At last the dead man walked no more
      Amongst the Trial Men,
And I knew that he was standing up
      In the black dock's dreadful pen,
And that never would I see his face
      In God's sweet world again.

Like two doomed ships that pass in storm
      We had crossed each other's way:
But we made no sign, we said no word,

We had no word to say;
For we did not meet in the holy night,
But in the shameful day.

A prison wall was round us both,
Two outcast men we were:
The world had thrust us from its heart,
And God from out His care:
And the iron gin that waits for Sin
Had caught us in its snare.

****

In Debtors' Yard the stones are hard,
And the dripping wall is high,
So it was there he took the air
Beneath the leaden sky,
And by each side a Warder walked,
For fear the man might die.

Or else he sat with those who watched
His anguish night and day;
Who watched him when he rose to weep,
And when he crouched to pray;
Who watched him lest himself should rob
Their scaffold of its prey.

****

And twice a day he smoked his pipe,
And drank his quart of beer:
His soul was resolute, and held
No hiding-place for fear;
He often said that he was glad
The hangman's hands were near.

But why he said so strange a thing
No Warder dared to ask:

For he to whom a watcher's doom
        Is given as his task,
Must set a lock upon his lips,
        And make his face a mask.

Or else he might be moved, and try
        To comfort or console:
And what should Human Pity do
        Pent up in Murderers' Hole?
What word of grace in such a place
        Could help a brother's soul?

                ****

We tore the tarry rope to shreds
        With blunt and bleeding nails;
We rubbed the doors, and scrubbed the floors,
        And cleaned the shining rails:
And, rank by rank, we soaped the plank,
        And clattered with the pails.

We sewed the sacks, we broke the stones,
        We turned the dusty drill:
We banged the tins, and bawled the hymns,
        And sweated on the mill:
But in the heart of every man
        Terror was lying still.

So still it lay that every day
        Crawled like a weed-clogged wave:
And we forgot the bitter lot
        That waits for fool and knave,
Till once, as we tramped in from work,
        We passed an open grave.

With yawning mouth the yellow hole
        Gaped for a living thing;
The very mud cried out for blood

To the thirsty asphalte ring:
And we knew that ere one dawn grew fair
Some prisoner had to swing.

Right in we went, with soul intent
On Death and Dread and Doom:
The hangman, with his little bag,
Went shuffling through the gloom:
And each man trembled as he crept
Into his numbered tomb.

****

That night the empty corridors
Were full of forms of Fear,
And up and down the iron town
Stole feet we could not hear,
And through the bars that hide the stars
White faces seemed to peer.

He lay as one who lies and dreams
In a pleasant meadow-land,
The watchers watched him as he slept,
And could not understand
How one could sleep so sweet a sleep
With a hangman close at hand.

But there is no sleep when men must weep
Who never yet have wept:
So we – the fool, the fraud, the knave –
That endless vigil kept,
And through each brain on hands of pain
Another's terror crept.

****

There is no chapel on the day
On which they hang a man:
The Chaplain's heart is far too sick,

Or his face is far too wan,
Or there is that written in his eyes
        Which none should look upon.

So they kept us close till nigh on noon,
        And then they rang the bell,
And the Warders with their jingling keys
        Opened each listening cell,
And down the iron stair we tramped,
        Each from his separate Hell.

Out into God's sweet air we went,
        But not in wonted way,
For this man's face was white with fear,
        And that man's face was gray,
And I never saw sad men who looked
        So wistfully at the day.

I never saw sad men who looked
        With such a wistful eye
Upon that little tent of blue
        We prisoners call the sky,
And at every careless cloud that passed
        In happy freedom by.

The Warders strutted up and down,
        And kept their herd of brutes,
Their uniforms were spick and span,
        And they wore their Sunday suits,
But we knew the work they had been at,
        By the quicklime on their boots.

For where a grave had opened wide,
        There was no grave at all:
Only a stretch of mud and sand
        By the hideous prison-wall,
And a little heap of burning lime,
        That the man should have his pall.

For three long years they will not sow
     Or root or seedling there:
For three long years the unblessed spot
     Will sterile be and bare,
And look upon the wondering sky
     With unreproachful stare.

They think a murderer's heart would taint
     Each simple seed they sow.
It is not true! God's kindly earth
     Is kindlier than men know,
And the red rose would but blow more red,
     The white rose whiter blow.

JOHN KEATS 1795–1821

TO AUTUMN

Season of mists and mellow fruitfulness,
    Close bosom-friend of the maturing sun;
Conspiring with him how to load and bless
    With fruit the vines that round the thatch-eaves run;
To bend with apples the mossed cottage-trees,
    And fill all fruit with ripeness to the core;
       To swell the gourd, and plump the hazel shells
    With a sweet kernel; to set budding more,
And still more, later flowers for the bees,
Until they think warm days will never cease,
    For Summer has o'er-brimmed their clammy cells.

Who hath not seen thee oft amid thy store?
    Sometimes whoever seeks abroad may find
Thee sitting careless on a granary floor,
    Thy hair soft-lifted by the winnowing wind;
Or on a half-reaped furrow sound asleep,
    Drowsed with the fumes of poppies, while thy hook
       Spares the next swath and all its twined flowers:
    And sometimes like a gleaner thou dost keep
Steady thy laden head across a brook;
Or by a cider-press, with patient look,
    Thou watchest the last oozings, hours by hours.

Where are the songs of Spring? Ay, where are they?
    Think not of them, thou hast thy music too –
While barred clouds bloom the soft-dying day,
    And touch the stubble-plains with rosy hue;
Then in a wailful choir the small gnats mourn
    Among the river sallows, borne aloft
       Or sinking as the light wind lives or dies;
    And full-grown lambs loud bleat from hilly bourn;
Hedge-crickets sing; and now with treble soft
The red-breast whistles from a garden croft;
    And gathering swallows twitter in the skies.

THE WASTE LAND

'Nam Sibyllam quidem Cumis ego ipse oculis meis
vidi in ampulla pendere, et cum illi pueri dicerent:
Sibylla ti theleis; respondebat illa: apothanein thelo.'

For Ezra Pound
il miglior fabbro

I. THE BURIAL OF THE DEAD

April is the cruellest month, breeding
Lilacs out of the dead land, mixing
Memory and desire, stirring
Dull roots with spring rain.
Winter kept us warm, covering
Earth in forgetful snow, feeding
A little life with dried tubers.
Summer surprised us, coming over the Starnbergersee
With a shower of rain; we stopped in the colonnade,
And went on in sunlight, into the Hofgarten,
And drank coffee, and talked for an hour.
Bin gar keine Russin, stamm' aus Litauen, echt deutsch.
And when we were children, staying at the archduke's,
My cousin's, he took me out on a sled,
And I was frightened. He said, Marie,
Marie, hold on tight. And down we went.
In the mountains, there you feel free.
I read, much of the night, and go south in the winter.

What are the roots that clutch, what branches grow
Out of this stony rubbish? Son of man,
You cannot say, or guess, for you know only
A heap of broken images, where the sun beats,

And the dead tree gives no shelter, the cricket no relief,
And the dry stone no sound of water. Only
There is shadow under this red rock,
(Come in under the shadow of this red rock),
And I will show you something different from either
Your shadow at morning striding behind you
Or your shadow at evening rising to meet you;
I will show you fear in a handful of dust.
                    Frisch weht der Wind
                    Der Heimat zu.
                    Mein Irisch Kind,
                    Wo weilest du?
'You gave me hyacinths first a year ago;
'They called me the hyacinth girl.'
— Yet when we came back, late, from the hyacinth garden,
Your arms full, and your hair wet, I could not
Speak, and my eyes failed, I was neither
Living nor dead, and I knew nothing,
Looking into the heart of light, the silence.
Oed' und leer das Meer.

Madame Sosostris, famous clairvoyante,
Had a bad cold, nevertheless
Is known to be the wisest woman in Europe,
With a wicked pack of cards. Here, said she,
Is your card, the drowned Phoenician Sailor,
(Those are pearls that were his eyes. Look!)
Here is Belladonna, the Lady of the Rocks,
The lady of situations.
Here is the man with three staves, and here the Wheel,
And here is the one-eyed merchant, and this card,
Which is blank, is something he carries on his back,
Which I am forbidden to see. I do not find
The Hanged Man. Fear death by water.
I see crowds of people, walking round in a ring.
Thank you. If you see dear Mrs. Equitone,

Tell her I bring the horoscope myself:
One must be so careful these days.

　　Unreal City,
Under the brown fog of a winter dawn,
A crowd flowed over London Bridge, so many,
I had not thought death had undone so many.
Sighs, short and infrequent, were exhaled,
And each man fixed his eyes before his feet.
Flowed up the hill and down King William Street,
To where Saint Mary Woolnoth kept the hours
With a dead sound on the final stroke of nine.
There I saw one I knew, and stopped him, crying 'Stetson!
'You who were with me in the ships at Mylae!
'That corpse you planted last year in your garden,
'Has it begun to sprout? Will it bloom this year?
'Or has the sudden frost disturbed its bed?
'Oh keep the Dog far hence, that's friend to men,
'Or with his nails he'll dig it up again!
'You! hypocrite lecteur! – mon semblable, – mon frère!'

II. A GAME OF CHESS

　　The Chair she sat in, like a burnished throne,
Glowed on the marble, where the glass
Held up by standards wrought with fruited vines
From which a golden Cupidon peeped out
(Another hid his eyes behind his wing)
Doubled the flames of sevenbranched candelabra
Reflecting light upon the table as
The glitter of her jewels rose to meet it,
From satin cases poured in rich profusion.
In vials of ivory and coloured glass
Unstoppered, lurked her strange synthetic perfumes,
Unguent, powdered, or liquid – troubled, confused
And drowned the sense in odours; stirred by the air

That freshened from the window, these ascended
In fattening the prolonged candle-flames,
Flung their smoke into the laquearia,
Stirring the pattern on the coffered ceiling.
Huge sea-wood fed with copper
Burned green and orange, framed by the coloured stone,
In which sad light a carved dolphin swam.
Above the antique mantel was displayed
As though a window gave upon the sylvan scene
The change of Philomel, by the barbarous king
So rudely forced; yet there the nightingale
Filled all the desert with inviolable voice
And still she cried, and still the world pursues,
'Jug Jug' to dirty ears.
And other withered stumps of time
Were told upon the walls; staring forms
Leaned out, leaning, hushing the room enclosed.
Footsteps shuffled on the stair.
Under the firelight, under the brush, her hair
Spread out in fiery points
Glowed into words, then would be savagely still.

'My nerves are bad to-night. Yes, bad. Stay with me.
'Speak to me. Why do you never speak? Speak.
'What are you thinking of? What thinking? What?
'I never know what you are thinking. Think.'

I think we are in rats' alley
Where the dead men lost their bones.

'What is that noise?
                    The wind under the door.
'What is that noise now? What is the wind doing?'
                    Nothing again nothing.
                                                    'Do
'You know nothing? Do you see nothing? Do you remember
'Nothing?'

130

I remember
Those are pearls that were his eyes.
'Are you alive, or not? Is there nothing in your head?'
                                        But

O O O O that Shakespeherian Rag –
It's so elegant
So intelligent
'What shall I do now? What shall I do?'
'I shall rush out as I am, and walk the street
'With my hair down, so. What shall we do to-morrow?
'What shall we ever do?'
                    The hot water at ten.
And if it rains, a closed car at four.
And we shall play a game of chess,
Pressing lidless eyes and waiting for a knock upon the door.

When Lil's husband got demobbed, I said –
I didn't mince my words, I said to her myself,
HURRY UP PLEASE IT'S TIME
Now Albert's coming back, make yourself a bit smart.
He'll want to know what you done with that money he gave you
To get yourself some teeth. He did, I was there.
You have them all out, Lil, and get a nice set,
He said, I swear, I can't bear to look at you.
And no more can't I, I said, and think of poor Albert,
He's been in the army four years, he wants a good time,
And if you don't give it him, there's others will, I said.
Oh is there, she said. Something o' that, I said.
Then I'll know who to thank, she said, and give me a straight look.
HURRY UP PLEASE IT'S TIME
If you don't like it you can get on with it, I said.
Others can pick and choose if you can't.
But if Albert makes off, it won't be for lack of telling.
You ought to be ashamed, I said, to look so antique.
(And her only thirty-one.)
I can't help it, she said, pulling a long face,

It's them pills I took, to bring it off, she said.
(She's had five already, and nearly died of young George.)
The chemist said it would be alright, but I've never been the same.
You *are* a proper fool, I said.
Well, if Albert won't leave you alone, there it is, I said,
What you get married for if you don't want children?
HURRY UP PLEASE IT'S TIME
Well, that Sunday Albert was home, they had a hot gammon,
And they asked me in to dinner, to get the beauty of it hot —
HURRY UP PLEASE IT'S TIME
HURRY UP PLEASE IT'S TIME
Goonight Bill. Goonight Lou. Goonight May. Goonight.
Ta ta. Goonight. Goonight.
Good night, ladies, good night, sweet ladies, good night, good night.

III. THE FIRE SERMON

    The river's tent is broken: the last fingers of leaf
Clutch and sink into the wet bank. The wind
Crosses the brown land, unheard. The nymphs are departed.
Sweet Thames, run softly, till I end my song.
The river bears no empty bottles, sandwich papers,
Silk handkerchiefs, cardboard boxes, cigarette ends
Or other testimony of summer nights. The nymphs are departed.
And their friends, the loitering heirs of city directors;
Departed, have left no addresses.
By the waters of Leman I sat down and wept . . .
Sweet Thames, run softly till I end my song,
Sweet Thames, run softly, for I speak not loud or long.
But at my back in a cold blast I hear
The rattle of the bones, and chuckle spread from ear to ear.

A rat crept softly through the vegetation
Dragging its slimy belly on the bank
While I was fishing in the dull canal
On a winter evening round behind the gashouse

Musing upon the king my brother's wreck
And on the king my father's death before him.
White bodies naked on the low damp ground
And bones cast in a little low dry garret,
Rattled by the rat's foot only, year to year.
But at my back from time to time I hear
The sound of horns and motors, which shall bring
Sweeney to Mrs. Porter in the spring.
O the moon shone bright on Mrs. Porter
And on her daughter
They wash their feet in soda water
Et O ces voix d'enfants, chantant dans la coupole!

Twit twit twit
Jug jug jug jug jug jug
So rudely forc'd.
Tereu

  Unreal City
Under the brown fog of a winter noon
Mr. Eugenides, the Smyrna merchant
Unshaven, with a pocket full of currants
C.i.f. London: documents at sight,
Asked me in demotic French
To luncheon at the Cannon Street Hotel
Followed by a weekend at the Metropole.

  At the violet hour, when the eyes and back
Turn upward from the desk, when the human engine waits
Like a taxi throbbing waiting,
I Tiresias, though blind, throbbing between two lives,
Old man with wrinkled female breasts, can see
At the violet hour, the evening hour that strives
Homeward, and brings the sailor home from sea,
The typist home at teatime, clears her breakfast, lights
Her stove, and lays out food in tins.

Out of the window perilously spread
Her drying combinations touched by the sun's last rays,
On the divan are piled (at night her bed)
Stockings, slippers, camisoles, and stays.
I Tiresias, old man with wrinkled dugs
Perceived the scene, and foretold the rest —
I too awaited the expected guest.
He, the young man carbuncular, arrives,
A small house agent's clerk, with one bold stare,
One of the low on whom assurance sits
As a silk hat on a Bradford millionaire.
The time is now propitious, as he guesses,
The meal is ended, she is bored and tired,
Endeavours to engage her in caresses
Which still are unreproved, if undesired.
Flushed and decided, he assaults at once;
Exploring hands encounter no defence;
His vanity requires no response,
And makes a welcome of indifference.
(And I Tiresias have foresuffered all
Enacted on this same divan or bed;
I who have sat by Thebes below the wall
And walked among the lowest of the dead.)
Bestows one final patronising kiss,
And gropes his way, finding the stairs unlit . . .

    She turns and looks a moment in the glass,
Hardly aware of her departed lover;
Her brain allows one half-formed thought to pass:
'Well now that's done: and I'm glad it's over.'
When lovely woman stoops to folly and
Paces about her room again, alone,
She smoothes her hair with automatic hand,
And puts a record on the gramophone.

'This music crept by me upon the waters'
And along the Strand, up Queen Victoria Street.
O City city, I can sometimes hear
Beside a public bar in Lower Thames Street,
The pleasant whining of a mandoline
And a clatter and a chatter from within
Where fishmen lounge at noon: where the walls
Of Magnus Martyr hold
Inexplicable splendour of Ionian white and gold.

      The river sweats
      Oil and tar
      The barges drift
      With the turning tide
      Red sails
      Wide
      To leeward, swing on the heavy spar.
      The barges wash
      Drifting logs
      Down Greenwich reach
      Past the Isle of Dogs.
            Weialala leia
            Wallala leialala

      Elizabeth and Leicester
      Beating oars
      The stern was formed
      A gilded shell
      Red and gold
      The brisk swell
      Rippled both shores
      Southwest wind
      Carried down stream
      The peal of bells
      White towers
            Weialala leia
            Wallala leialala

'Trams and dusty trees.
Highbury bore me. Richmond and Kew
Undid me. By Richmond I raised my knees
Supine on the floor of a narrow canoe.'
'My feet are at Moorgate, and my heart
Under my feet. After the event
He wept. He promised 'a new start'.
I made no comment. What should I resent?'
'On Margate Sands.
I can connect
Nothing with nothing.
The broken fingernails of dirty hands.
My people humble people who expect
Nothing.'
         la la

To Carthage then I came

Burning burning burning burning
O Lord Thou pluckest me out
O Lord Thou pluckest

burning

IV. DEATH BY WATER

Phlebas the Phoenician, a fortnight dead,
Forgot the cry of gulls, and the deep seas swell
And the profit and loss.
                     A current under sea
Picked his bones in whispers. As he rose and fell
He passed the stages of his age and youth
Entering the whirlpool.
                   Gentile or Jew
O you who turn the wheel and look to windward,
Consider Phlebas, who was once handsome and tall as you.

V. WHAT THE THUNDER SAID

After the torchlight red on sweaty faces
After the frosty silence in the gardens
After the agony in stony places
The shouting and the crying
Prison and palace and reverberation
Of thunder of spring over distant mountains
He who was living is now dead
We who were living are now dying
With a little patience

Here is no water but only rock
Rock and no water and the sandy road
The road winding above among the mountains
Which are mountains of rock without water
If there were water we should stop and drink
Amongst the rock one cannot stop or think
Sweat is dry and feet are in the sand
If there were only water amongst the rock
Dead mountain mouth of carious teeth that cannot spit
Here one can neither stand nor lie nor sit
There is not even silence in the mountains
But dry sterile thunder without rain
There is not even solitude in the mountains
But red sullen faces sneer and snarl
From doors of mudcracked houses
                    If there were water
    And no rock
    If there were rock
    And also water
    And water
    A spring
    A pool among the rock
    If there were the sound of water only
    Not the cicada

137

And dry grass singing
But sound of water over a rock
Where the hermit-thrush sings in the pine trees
Drip drop drip drop drop drop drop
But there is no water

    Who is the third who walks always beside you?
When I count, there are only you and I together
But when I look ahead up the white road
There is always another one walking beside you
Gliding wrapt in a brown mantle, hooded
I do not know whether a man or a woman
– But who is that on the other side of you?

    What is that sound high in the air
Murmur of maternal lamentation
Who are those hooded hordes swarming
Over endless plains, stumbling in cracked earth
Ringed by the flat horizon only
What is the city over the mountains
Cracks and reforms and bursts in the violet air
Falling towers
Jerusalem Athens Alexandria
Vienna London
Unreal

A woman drew her long black hair out tight
And fiddled whisper music on those strings
And bats with baby faces in the violet light
Whistled, and beat their wings
And crawled head downward down a blackened wall
And upside down in air were towers
Tolling reminiscent bells, that kept the hours
And voices singing out of empty cisterns and exhausted wells.

In this decayed hole among the mountains
In the faint moonlight, the grass is singing
Over the tumbled graves, about the chapel
There is the empty chapel, only the wind's home.
It has no windows, and the door swings,
Dry bones can harm no one.
Only a cock stood on the rooftree
Co co rico co co rico
In a flash of lightning. Then a damp gust
Bringing rain

Ganga was sunken, and the limp leaves
Waited for rain, while the black clouds
Gathered far distant, over Himavant.
The jungle crouched, humped in silence.
Then spoke the thunder
DA
Datta: what have we given?
My friend, blood shaking my heart
The awful daring of a moment's surrender
Which an age of prudence can never retract
By this, and this only, we have existed
Which is not to be found in our obituaries
Or in memories draped by the beneficent spider
Or under seals broken by the lean solicitor
In our empty rooms
DA
Dayadhvam: I have heard the key
Turn in the door once and turn once only
We think of the key, each in his prison
Thinking of the key, each confirms a prison
Only at nightfall, aetherial rumours
Revive for a moment a broken Coriolanus
DA
Damyata: The boat responded
Gaily, to the hand expert with sail and oar

The sea was calm, your heart would have responded
Gaily, when invited, beating obedient
To controlling hands

                    I sat upon the shore
Fishing, with the arid plain behind me
Shall I at least set my lands in order?
London Bridge is falling down falling down falling down

Poi s'ascose nel foco che gli affina
Quando fiam ceu chelidon — O swallow swallow
Le Prince d'Aquitaine à la tour abolie
These fragments I have shored against my ruins
Why then Ile fit you. Hieronymo's mad againe.
Datta. Dayadhvam. Damyata.
             Shantih shantih shantih

JAMES K. BAXTER 1926–72

BALLAD OF CALVARY STREET

On Calvary Street are trellises
Where bright as blood the roses bloom,
And gnomes like pagan fetishes
Hang their hats on an empty tomb
Where two old souls go slowly mad,
National Mum and Labour Dad.

Each Saturday when full of smiles
The children come to pay their due,
Mum takes down the family files
And cover to cover she thumbs them through,
Poor Len before he went away
And Mabel on her wedding day.

The meal-brown scones display her knack,
Her polished oven spits with rage,
While in Grunt Grotto at the back
Dad sits and reads the Sporting Page,
Then ambles out in boots of lead
To weed around the parsnip bed.

A giant parsnip sparks his eye,
Majestic as the Tree of Life:
He washes it and rubs it dry
And takes it in to his old wife –
'Look Laura, would that be a fit?
The bastard has a flange on it!'

When both were young she would have laughed,
A goddess in her tartan skirt,
But wisdom, age and mothercraft
Have rubbed it home that men like dirt:
Five children and a fallen womb,
A golden crown beyond the tomb.

Nearer the bone, sin is sin,
And women bear the cross of woe,
And that affair with Mrs. Flynn
(It happened thirty years ago)
Though never mentioned, means that he
Will get no sugar in his tea.

The afternoon goes by, goes by,
The angels harp above a cloud,
A son-in-law with spotted tie
And daughter Alice fat and loud
Discuss the virtues of insurance
And stuff their tripes with trained endurance.

Flood-waters hurl upon the dyke
And Dad himself can go to town,
For little Charlie on his trike
Has ploughed another iris down.
His parents rise to chain the beast,
Brush off the last crumbs of their lovefeast.

And so these two old fools are left,
A rosy pair in evening light,
To question Heaven's dubious gift,
To hag and grumble, growl and fight:
The love they kill won't let them rest,
Two birds that peck in one fouled nest.

Why hammer nails? Why give no change?
Habit, habit clogs them dumb.
The Sacred Heart above the range
Will bleed and burn till Kingdom Come,
But Yin and Yang won't ever meet
In Calvary Street, in Calvary Street.

MAYA ANGELOU 1928–

STILL I RISE

You may write me down in history
With your bitter, twisted lies,
You may trod me in the very dirt
But still, like dust, I'll rise.

Does my sassiness upset you?
Why are you beset with gloom?
'Cause I walk like I've got oil wells
Pumping in my living room.

Just like moons and like suns,
With the certainty of tides,
Just like hopes springing high,
Still I'll rise.

Did you want to see me broken?
Bowed head and lowered eyes?
Shoulders falling down like teardrops.
Weakened by my soulful cries.

Does my haughtiness offend you?
Don't you take it awful hard
'Cause I laugh like I've got gold mines
Diggin' in my own back yard.

You may shoot me with your words,
You may cut me with your eyes,
You may kill me with your hatefulness,
But still, like air, I'll rise.

Does my sexiness upset you?
Does it come as a surprise
That I dance like I've got diamonds
At the meeting of my thighs?

Out of the huts of history's shame
I rise
Up from a past that's rooted in pain
I rise
I'm a black ocean, leaping and wide,
Welling and swelling I bear in the tide.
Leaving behind nights of terror and fear
I rise
Into a daybreak that's wondrously clear
I rise
Bringing the gifts that my ancestors gave,
I am the dream and the hope of the slave.
I rise
I rise
I rise.

MUSÉE DES BEAUX ARTS

About suffering they were never wrong,
The Old Masters: how well they understood
Its human position; how it takes place
While someone else is eating or opening a window or just walking dully along;
How, when the aged are reverently, passionately waiting
For the miraculous birth, there always must be
Children who did not specially want it to happen, skating
On a pond at the edge of the wood:
They never forgot
That even the dreadful martyrdom must run its course
Anyhow in a corner, some untidy spot
Where the dogs go on with their doggy life and the torturer's horse
Scratches its innocent behind on a tree.

In Brueghel's Icarus for instance: how everything turns away
Quite leisurely from the disaster; the ploughman may
Have heard the splash, the forsaken cry,
But for him it was not an important failure; the sun shone
As it had to on the white legs disappearing into the green
Water; and the expensive delicate ship that must have seen
Something amazing, a boy falling out of the sky,
Had somewhere to get to and sailed calmly on.

PHILIP LARKIN 1922–85

THIS BE THE VERSE

They fuck you up, your mum and dad.
    They may not mean to, but they do.
They fill you with the faults they had
    And add some extra, just for you.

But they were fucked up in their turn
    By fools in old-style hats and coats,
Who half the time were soppy-stern
    And half at one another's throats.

Man hands on misery to man.
    It deepens like a coastal shelf.
Get out as early as you can,
    And don't have any kids yourself.

G. K. CHESTERTON 1874–1936

THE DONKEY

When fishes flew and forests walked
  And figs grew upon thorn,
Some moment when the moon was blood
  Then surely I was born.

With monstrous head and sickening cry
  And ears like errant wings,
The devil's walking parody
  On all four-footed things.

The tattered outlaw of the earth,
  Of ancient crooked will;
Starve, scourge, deride me: I am dumb,
  I keep my secret still.

Fools! For I also had my hour;
  One far fierce hour and sweet:
There was a shout about my ears,
  And palms before my feet.

ROBERT BURNS 1759–96

TO A MOUSE
On Turning Her Up in Her Nest With the Plough

Wee, sleekit, cow'rin, tim'rous beastie,
O, what a panic's in thy breastie!
Thou need na start awa sae hasty,
   Wi' bickering brattle!
I wad be laith to rin an' chase thee,
   Wi' murd'ring pattle!

I'm truly sorry man's dominion,
Has broken nature's social union,
An' justifies that ill opinion,
   Which makes thee startle
At me, thy poor, earth-born companion,
   An' fellow-mortal!

I doubt na, whiles, but thou may thieve;
What then? poor beastie, thou maun live!
A daimen icker in a thrave
   'S a sma' request;
I'll get a blessin wi' the lave,
   An' never miss't!

Thy wee bit housie, too, in ruin!
It's silly wa's the win's are strewin!
An' naething, now, to big a new ane,
   O' foggage green!
An' bleak December's winds ensuin,
   Baith snell an' keen!

Thou saw the fields laid bare an' waste,
An' weary winter comin fast,
An' cozie here, beneath the blast,
    Thou thought to dwell —
Till crash! the cruel coulter past
    Out thro' thy cell.

That wee bit heap o' leaves an' stibble,
Has cost thee mony a weary nibble!
Now thou's turn'd out, for a' thy trouble,
    But house or hald,
To thole the winter's sleety dribble,
An' cranreuch cauld!

But, Mousie, thou art no thy lane,
In proving foresight may be vain;
The best-laid schemes o' mice an' men
    Gang aft agley,
An' lea'e us nought but grief an' pain,
    For promis'd joy!

Still thou art blest, compar'd wi' me
The present only toucheth thee:
But, Och! I backward cast my e'e,
    On prospects drear!
An' forward, tho' I canna see,
    I guess an' fear!

OH, I WISH I'D LOOKED AFTER ME TEETH

Oh, I wish I'd looked after me teeth,
And spotted the perils beneath,
All the toffees I chewed,
And the sweet sticky food,
Oh, I wish I'd looked after me teeth.
When I had more tooth there than fillin'
To pass up gobstoppers,
From respect to me choppers
And to buy something else with me shillin'.

When I think of the lollies I licked,
And the liquorice allsorts I picked,
Sherbet dabs, big and little,
All that hard peanut brittle,
My conscience gets horribly pricked.

My Mother, she told me no end,
'If you got a tooth, you got a friend.'
I was young then, and careless,
My toothbrush was hairless,
I never had much time to spend.

Oh I showed them the toothpaste all right,
I flashed it about late at night,
But up-and-down brushin'
And pokin' and fussin'
Didn't seem worth the time... I could bite!

If I'd known I was paving the way,
To cavities, caps and decay,
The murder of fillin's
Injections and drillin's
I'd have thrown all me sherbet away.

So I lay in the old dentist's chair,
And I gaze up his nose in despair,
And his drill it do whine,
In these molars of mine,
'Two amalgam,' he'll say, 'for in there.'

How I laughed at my Mother's false teeth,
As they foamed in the waters beneath,
But now comes the reckonin'
It's *me* they are beckonin'
Oh, I *wish* I'd looked after me teeth.

ROBERT BURNS 1759–96

A RED, RED ROSE

TUNE: MAJOR GRAHAM

O my luve's like a red, red rose,
 That's newly sprung in June;
O my luve's like the melodie
 That's sweetly play'd in tune.

As fair art thou, my bonie lass,
 So deep in luve am I,
And I will luve thee still, my Dear,
 Till a' the seas gang dry.

Till a' the seas gang dry, my Dear,
 And the rocks melt wi' the sun:
I will luve thee still, my Dear,
 While the sands o' life shall run.

And fare thee weel, my only Luve,
 And fare thee weel a while!
And I will come again, my Luve,
 Tho' it were ten thousand mile!

EMILY DICKINSON 1830–86

BECAUSE I COULD NOT STOP FOR DEATH

Because I could not stop for death,
He kindly stopped for me;
The carriage held but just ourselves
And immortality.

We slowly drove, he knew no haste,
And I had put away
My labour, and my leisure too,
For his civility.

We passed the school, where children strove
At recess, in the ring;
We passed the fields of gazing grain,
We passed the setting sun.

Or rather, he passed us;
The dews drew quivering and chill,
For only gossamer my gown,
My tippet only tulle.

We paused before a house that seemed
A swelling of the ground;
The roof was scarcely visible,
The cornice in the ground.

Since then 'tis centuries, and yet
Feels shorter than the day
I first surmised the horses' heads
Were toward eternity.

KIT WRIGHT 1944–

GREEDYGUTS

I sat in the café and sipped at a Coke.
There sat down beside me a WHOPPING great bloke
Who sighed as he elbowed me into the wall:
'Your trouble, my boy, is your belly's too small!
Your bottom's too thin! Take a lesson from me:
I may not be nice, but I'm GREAT, you'll agree,
And I've lasted a lifetime by playing this hunch:
The bigger the breakfast, the larger the lunch!

The larger the lunch, then the huger the supper.
The deeper the teapot, the vaster the cupper.
The fatter the sausage, the fuller the tea.
The MORE on the table, the BETTER FOR ME!'

His elbows moved in and his elbows moved out,
His belly grew bigger, chins wobbled about,
As forkful by forkful and plate after plate,
He ate and he ate and he ate and he ATE!

I hardly could breathe, I was squashed out of shape,
So under the table I made my escape.
'Aha!' he rejoiced, 'when it's put to the test,
The fellow who's fattest will come off the best!
Remember, my boy, when it comes to the crunch:
The bigger the breakfast, the larger the lunch!

The larger the lunch, then the huger the supper.
The deeper the teapot, the vaster the cupper.
The fatter the sausage, the fuller the tea.
The MORE on the table, the BETTER FOR ME!'

A lady came by who was scrubbing the floor
With a mop and a bucket. To even the score,
I lifted that bucket of water and said,
As I poured the whole lot of it over his head:

'I've found all my life, it's a pretty sure bet:
The FULLER the bucket, the WETTER YOU GET!'

ALFRED, LORD TENNYSON 1809–92

ULYSSES

It little profits that an idle king,
By this still hearth, among these barren crags,
Match'd with an aged wife, I mete and dole
Unequal laws unto a savage race,
That hoard, and sleep, and feed, and know not me.
I cannot rest from travel: I will drink
Life to the lees: all times I have enjoy'd
Greatly, have suffer'd greatly, both with those
That loved me, and alone; on shore, and when
Thro' scudding drifts the rainy Hyades
Vext the dim sea: I am become a name;
For always roaming with a hungry heart
Much have I seen and known; cities of men
And manners, climates, councils, governments,
Myself not least, but honour'd of them all;
And drunk delight of battle with my peers,
Far on the ringing plains of windy Troy.
I am a part of all that I have met;
Yet all experience is an arch wherethro'
Gleams that untravell'd world, whose margin fades
For ever and for ever when I move.
How dull it is to pause, to make an end,
To rust unburnish'd, not to shine in use!
As tho' to breathe were life. Life piled on life
Were all too little, and of one to me
Little remains: but every hour is saved
From that eternal silence, something more,
A bringer of new things; and vile it were
For some three suns to store and hoard myself,
And this grey spirit yearning in desire
To follow knowledge, like a sinking star,
Beyond the utmost bound of human thought.
    This is my son, mine own Telemachus,

To whom I leave the sceptre and the isle —
Well-loved of me, discerning to fulfil
This labour, by slow prudence to make mild
A rugged people, and thro' soft degrees
Subdue them to the useful and the good.
Most blameless is he, centred in the sphere
Of common duties, decent not to fail
In offices of tenderness, and pay
Meet adoration to my household gods,
When I am gone. He works his work, I mine.

   There lies the port: the vessel puffs her sail:
There gloom the dark broad seas. My mariners,
Souls that have toil'd, and wrought, and thought with me —
That ever with a frolic welcome took
The thunder and the sunshine, and opposed
Free hearts, free foreheads — you and I are old;
Old age hath yet his honour and his toil;
Death closes all: but something ere the end,
Some work of noble note, may yet be done,
Not unbecoming men that strove with Gods.
The lights begin to twinkle from the rocks:
The long day wanes: the slow moon climbs: the deep
Moans round with many voices. Come, my friends,
'Tis not too late to seek a newer world.
Push off, and sitting well in order smite
The sounding furrows; for my purpose holds
To sail beyond the sunset, and the baths
Of all the western stars, until I die.
It may be that the gulfs will wash us down:
It may be we shall touch the Happy Isles,
And see the great Achilles, whom we knew.
Tho' much is taken, much abides; and tho'
We are not now that strength which in old days
Moved earth and heaven; that which we are, we are;
One equal temper of heroic hearts,
Made weak by time and fate, but strong in will
To strive, to seek, to find, and not to yield.

JOHN KEATS 1795–1821

ODE ON A GRECIAN URN

Thou still unravished bride of quietness,
   Thou foster-child of silence and slow time,
Sylvan historian, who canst thus express
   A flowery tale more sweetly than our rhyme:
What leaf-fringed legend haunts about thy shape
     Of deities or mortals, or of both,
       In Tempe or the dales of Arcady?
     What men or gods are these? What maidens loth?
What mad pursuit? What struggle to escape?
     What pipes and timbrels? What wild ecstasy?

Heard melodies are sweet, but those unheard
   Are sweeter; therefore, ye soft pipes, play on;
Not to the sensual ear, but, more endeared,
   Pipe to the spirit ditties of no tone:
Fair youth, beneath the trees, thou canst not leave
     Thy song, nor ever can those trees be bare;
       Bold Lover, never, never canst thou kiss,
Though winning near the goal – yet, do not grieve:
     She cannot fade, though thou hast not thy bliss,
   For ever wilt thou love, and she be fair!

Ah, happy, happy boughs! that cannot shed
   Your leaves, nor ever bid the Spring adieu;
And, happy melodist, unwearied,
   For ever piping songs for ever new;
More happy love! more happy, happy love!
     For ever warm and still to be enjoyed,
       For ever panting, and for ever young –
All breathing human passion far above,
     That leaves a heart high-sorrowful and cloyed,
   A burning forehead, and a parching tongue.

Who are these coming to the sacrifice?
　　To what green altar, O mysterious priest,
Lead'st thou that heifer lowing at the skies,
　　And all her silken flanks with garlands dressed?
What little town by river or sea shore,
　　Or mountain-built with peaceful citadel,
　　　　Is emptied of this folk, this pious morn?
And, little town, thy streets for evermore
　　Will silent be; and not a soul to tell
　　　　Why thou art desolate, can e'er return.

O Attic shape! Fair attitude! with brede
　　Of marble men and maidens overwrought,
With forest branches and the trodden weed;
　　Thou, silent form, dost tease us out of thought
As doth eternity: Cold Pastoral!
　　When old age shall this generation waste,
　　　　Thou shalt remain, in midst of other woe
　　Than ours, a friend to man, to whom thou say'st,
'Beauty is truth, truth beauty, – that is all
　　　　Ye know on earth, and all ye need to know.'

DENIS GLOVER 1912–80

From ARAWATA BILL

The Scene

Mountains nuzzle mountains
White-bearded rock-fronted
In perpetual drizzle.
Rivers swell and twist
Like a torturer's fist
Where the maidenhair
Falls of the waterfall
Sail through the air.

The mountains send below
Their cold tribute of snow
And the birch makes brown
The rivulets running down.

Rock, air and water meet
Where crags debate
The dividing cloud.

In the dominion of the thorn
The delicate cloud is born,
And golden nuggets bloom
In the womb of the storm.

Arawata Bill

With his weapon a shovel
To test the river gravel
His heart was as big as his boots
As he headed over the tops
In blue dungarees and a sunset hat.

Wicked country, but there might be
Gold in it for all that,

Under the shoulder of a boulder
Or in the darkened gully,
Fit enough country for
A blanket and a billy
Where nothing stirred
Under the cold eye of the bird.

Some climbers bivvy
Heavy with rope and primus.
But not so
Arawata Bill and the old-timers.

Some people shave in the mountains.
But not so
Arawata Bill who let his whiskers grow.

I met a man from the mountains
Who told me that Bill
Left cairns across the ravines
And through the scrub on the hill
— And they're there still.

And he found,
Together with a kea's feather,
A rusting shovel in the ground
By a derelict hovel.

It had been there long,
But the handle was good and strong.

The Search

What unknown affinity
Lies between mountain and sea
In country crumpled like an unmade bed
Whose crumbs may be nuggets as big as your head
And it's all snow-sheeted, storm-cloud fed?
    Far behind is the blue Pacific,
    And the Tasman somewhere ahead.

Wet or dry, low or high,
Somewhere in a blanketfold of the land
Lies the golden strand.

    Mountain spells may bind it,
    But the marrow in the bone
    The itch in the palm
    The Chinaman's talisman
    To save from harm,
    All tell me I shall find it.

These mountains never stir
In the still or turbulent air.
Only the stones thaw-loosened
Leap from the precipice
Into shrapnel snow-cushioned.

    An egg-timer shingle-fan
    Dribbles into the pan
    And the river sluices with many voices.

The best pan is an old pan
— The grains cling to the rust,
And a few will come from each panning,
The rust brown, and golden the dust.

But where is the amethyst sky and the high
Mountain of pure gold?

A Prayer

Mother of God, in this brazen sun
Lead me down from the arid heights
Before my strength is done.
Give me the rain
That not long since I cursed in vain.
Lead me to the river, the life-giver.

A Question

Who felled that tree,
And whose lean-to
Is melting now into that snow?

Barrington or Douglas perhaps
Left these faint tracks
As I, Bill,
Leave my cairns on the hill.

But the mountains on the rim of day
Have nothing to say.
Am I stealing their gold
As a gypsy steals a child,
Am I frisking their petticoats
Camping in the wild?

What do the peaks prepare
For a usurper camping
Where they hold the air
And the river-bend no friend?

The River Crossing

The river was announcing
An ominous crossing
With the boulders knocking.

'You can do it and make a fight of it,
Always taking the hard way
For the hell and delight of it.

But there comes the day
When you watch the spate of it,
And camp till the moon's down
— Then find the easy way

Across in the dawn,
Waiting till that swollen vein
Of a river subsides again.'

And Bill set up his camp and watched
His young self, river-cold and scratched,
Struggling across, and up the wrong ridge,
And turning back, temper on edge.

MAX EHRMANN 1872–1945

DESIDERATA

Go placidly amid the noise and haste,
and remember what peace there may be in silence.
As far as possible without surrender
be on good terms with all persons.
Speak your truth quietly and clearly;
and listen to others,
even the dull and the ignorant;
they too have their story.

Avoid loud and aggressive persons,
they are vexations to the spirit.
If you compare yourself with others,
you may become vain and bitter;
for always there will be greater and lesser persons than yourself.
Enjoy your achievements as well as your plans.

Keep interested in your own career, however humble;
it is a real possession in the changing fortunes of time.
Exercise caution in your business affairs;
for the world is full of trickery.
But let this not blind you to what virtue there is;
many persons strive for high ideals;
and everywhere life is full of heroism.

Be yourself.
Especially, do not feign affection.
Neither be cynical about love;
for in the face of all aridity and disenchantment
it is as perennial as the grass.

Take kindly the counsel of the years,
gracefully surrendering the things of youth.
Nurture strength of spirit to shield you in sudden misfortune.
But do not distress yourself with dark imaginings.
Many fears are born of fatigue and loneliness.
Beyond a wholesome discipline,
be gentle with yourself.

You are a child of the universe,
no less than the trees and the stars;
you have a right to be here.
And whether or not it is clear to you,
no doubt the universe is unfolding as it should.

Therefore be at peace with God,
whatever you conceive Him to be,
and whatever your labors and aspirations,
in the noisy confusion of life keep peace with your soul.

With all its sham, drudgery, and broken dreams,
it is still a beautiful world.
Be cheerful.
Strive to be happy.

T.S. ELIOT 1888–1965

LITTLE GIDDING

I

Midwinter spring is its own season
Sempiternal though sodden towards sundown,
Suspended in time, between pole and tropic.
When the short day is brightest, with frost and fire,
The brief sun flames the ice, on pond and ditches,
In windless cold that is the heart's heat,
Reflecting in a watery mirror
A glare that is blindness in the early afternoon
And glow more intense than blaze of branch, or brazier.
Stirs the dumb spirit: no wind, but pentecostal fire
In the dark time of the year. Between melting and freezing
The soul's sap quivers. There is no earth smell
Or smell of living thing. This is the spring time
But not in time's covenant. Now the hedgerow
Is blanched for an hour with transitory blossom
Of snow, a bloom more sudden
Than that of summer, neither budding nor fading,
Not in the scheme of generation.
Where is the summer, the unimaginable
Zero summer?

　　　　If you came this way,
Taking the route you would be likely to take
From the place you would be likely to come from,
If you came this way in may time, you would find the hedges
White again, in May, with voluptuary sweetness.
It would be the same at the end of the journey,
If you came at night like a broken king,
If you came by day not knowing what you came for,
It would be the same, when you leave the rough road
And turn behind the pig-sty to the dull facade
And the tombstone. And what you thought you came for

Is only a shell, a husk of meaning
From which the purpose breaks only when it is fulfilled
If at all. Either you had no purpose
Or the purpose is beyond the end you figured
And is altered in fulfilment. There are other places
Which also are the world's end, some at the sea jaws,
Or over a dark lake, in a desert or a city —
But this is the nearest, in place and time,
Now and in England.

    If you came this way,
Taking any route, starting from anywhere,
At any time or at any season,
It would always be the same: you would have to put off
Sense and notion. You are not here to verify,
Instruct yourself, or inform curiosity
Or carry report. You are here to kneel
Where prayer has been valid. And prayer is more
Than an order of words, the conscious occupation
Of the praying mind, or the sound of the voice praying.
And what the dead had no speech for, when living,
They can tell you, being dead: the communication
Of the dead is tongued with fire beyond the language of the living.
Here, the intersection of the timeless moment
Is England and nowhere. Never and always.

II

Ash on an old man's sleeve
Is all the ash the burnt roses leave.
Dust in the air suspended
Marks the place where a story ended.
Dust inbreathed was a house —
The walls, the wainscot and the mouse,
The death of hope and despair,
  This is the death of air.

There are flood and drouth
Over the eyes and in the mouth,
Dead water and dead sand
Contending for the upper hand.
The parched eviscerate soil
Gapes at the vanity of toil,
Laughs without mirth.
    This is the death of earth.

Water and fire succeed
The town, the pasture and the weed.
Water and fire deride
The sacrifice that we denied.
Water and fire shall rot
The marred foundations we forgot,
Of sanctuary and choir.
    This is the death of water and fire.

In the uncertain hour before the morning
    Near the ending of interminable night
    At the recurrent end of the unending
After the dark dove with the flickering tongue
    Had passed below the horizon of his homing
    While the dead leaves still rattled on like tin
Over the asphalt where no other sound was
    Between three districts whence the smoke arose
    I met one walking, loitering and hurried
As if blown towards me like the metal leaves
    Before the urban dawn wind unresisting.
    And as I fixed upon the down-turned face
That pointed scrutiny with which we challenge
    The first-met stranger in the waning dusk
    I caught the sudden look of some dead master
Whom I had known, forgotten, half recalled
    Both one and many; in the brown baked features
    The eyes of a familiar compound ghost
Both intimate and unidentifiable.

So I assumed a double part, and cried
And heard another's voice cry: 'What! are *you* here?'
Although we were not. I was still the same,
Knowing myself yet being someone other —
And he a face still forming; yet the words sufficed
To compel the recognition they preceded.
And so, compliant to the common wind,
Too strange to each other for misunderstanding,
In concord at this intersection time
Of meeting nowhere, no before and after,
We trod the pavement in a dead patrol.
I said: 'The wonder that I feel is easy,
Yet ease is cause of wonder. Therefore speak:
I may not comprehend, may not remember.'
And he: 'I am not eager to rehearse
My thoughts and theory which you have forgotten.
These things have served their purpose: let them be.
So with your own, and pray they be forgiven
By others, as I pray you to forgive
Both bad and good. Last season's fruit is eaten
And the fullfed beast shall kick the empty pail.
For last year's words belong to last year's language
And next year's words await another voice.
But, as the passage now presents no hindrance
To the spirit unappeased and peregrine
Between two worlds become much like each other,
So I find words I never thought to speak
In streets I never thought I should revisit
When I left my body on a distant shore.
Since our concern was speech, and speech impelled us
To purify the dialect of the tribe
And urge the mind to aftersight and foresight,
Let me disclose the gifts reserved for age
To set a crown upon your lifetime's effort.
First, the cold friction of expiring sense
Without enchantment, offering no promise

But bitter tastelessness of shadow fruit
As body and soul begin to fall asunder.
Second, the conscious impotence of rage
At human folly, and the laceration
Of laughter at what ceases to amuse.
And last, the rending pain of re-enactment
Of all that you have done, and been; the shame
Of motives late revealed, and the awareness
Of things ill done and done to others' harm
Which once you took for exercise of virtue.
Then fools' approval stings, and honour stains.
From wrong to wrong the exasperated spirit
Proceeds, unless restored by that refining fire
Where you must move in measure, like a dancer.'
The day was breaking. In the disfigured street
He left me, with a kind of valediction,
And faded on the blowing of the horn.

III

There are three conditions which often look alike
Yet differ completely, flourish in the same hedgerow:
Attachment to self and to things and to persons, detachment
From self and from things and from persons; and, growing between
them, indifference
Which resembles the others as death resembles life,
Being between two lives – unflowering, between
The live and the dead nettle. This is the use of memory:
For liberation – not less of love but expanding
Of love beyond desire, and so liberation
From the future as well as the past. Thus, love of a country
Begins as attachment to our own field of action
And comes to find that action of little importance
Though never indifferent. History may be servitude,
History may be freedom. See, now they vanish,
The faces and places, with the self which, as it could, loved them,

To become renewed, transfigured, in another pattern.
Sin is Behovely, but
All shall be well, and
All manner of thing shall be well.
If I think, again, of this place,
And of people, not wholly commendable,
Of no immediate kin or kindness,
But of some peculiar genius,
All touched by a common genius,
United in the strife which divided them;
If I think of a king at nightfall,
Of three men, and more, on the scaffold
And a few who died forgotten
In other places, here and abroad,
And of one who died blind and quiet
Why should we celebrate
These dead men more than the dying?
It is not to ring the bell backward
Nor is it an incantation
To summon the spectre of a Rose.
We cannot revive old factions
We cannot restore old policies
Or follow an antique drum.
These men, and those who opposed them
And those whom they opposed
Accept the constitution of silence
And are folded in a single party.
Whatever we inherit from the fortunate
We have taken from the defeated
What they had to leave us – a symbol:
A symbol perfected in death.
And all shall be well and
All manner of thing shall be well
By the purification of the motive
In the ground of our beseeching.

IV

The dove descending breaks the air
With flame of incandescent terror
Of which the tongues declare
The one discharge from sin and error.
The only hope, or else despair
    Lies in the choice of pyre of pyre –
    To be redeemed from fire by fire.

Who then devised the torment? Love.
Love is the unfamiliar Name
Behind the hands that wove
The intolerable shirt of flame
Which human power cannot remove.
    We only live, only suspire
    Consumed by either fire or fire.

V

What we call the beginning is often the end
And to make an end is to make a beginning.
The end is where we start from. And every phrase
And sentence that is right (where every word is at home,
Taking its place to support the others,
The word neither diffident nor ostentatious,
An easy commerce of the old and the new,
The common word exact without vulgarity,
The formal word precise but not pedantic,
The complete consort dancing together)
Every phrase and every sentence is an end and a beginning,
Every poem an epitaph. And any action
Is a step to the block, to the fire, down the sea's throat
Or to an illegible stone: and that is where we start.
We die with the dying:
See, they depart, and we go with them.

We are born with the dead:
See, they return, and bring us with them.
The moment of the rose and the moment of the yew-tree
Are of equal duration. A people without history
Is not redeemed from time, for history is a pattern
Of timeless moments. So, while the light fails
On a winter's afternoon, in a secluded chapel
History is now and England.

With the drawing of this Love and the voice of this
   Calling

We shall not cease from exploration
And the end of all our exploring
Will be to arrive where we started
And know the place for the first time.
Through the unknown, unremembered gate
When the last of earth left to discover
Is that which was the beginning;
At the source of the longest river
The voice of the hidden waterfall
And the children in the apple-tree
Not known, because not looked for
But heard, half-heard, in the stillness
Between two waves of the sea.
Quick now, here, now, always —
A condition of complete simplicity
(Costing not less than everything)
And all shall be well and
All manner of thing shall be well
When the tongues of flame are in-folded
Into the crowned knot of fire
And the fire and the rose are one.

SAM HUNT 1946–

PORIRUA FRIDAY NIGHT

Acne blossoms scarlet on their cheeks
These kids up Porirua East....
Pinned across this young girl's breast
A name-tag on the supermarket badge;
A city-sky-blue smock.
Her face unclenches like a fist.

Fourteen when I met her first
A year ago, she's now left school,
Going with the boy
She hopes will marry her next year.
I asked if she found it hard
Working in the store these Friday nights
When friends are on the town.

She never heard;
But went on, rather, talking of
The house her man had put
A first deposit on
And what it's like to be in love.

RUDYARD KIPLING 1865–1936

A SMUGGLER'S SONG
'Hal o' the Draft'

If you wake at midnight, and hear a horse's feet,
Don't go drawing back the blind, or looking in the street,
Them that ask no questions isn't told a lie.
Watch the wall, my darling, while the Gentlemen go by!
   Five and twenty ponies,
   Trotting through the dark –
   Brandy for the Parson,
   'Baccy for the Clerk;
   Laces for a lady, letters for a spy,
And watch the wall, my darling, while the Gentlemen go by!

Running round the woodlump if you chance to find
Little barrels, roped and tarred, all full of brandy-wine,
Don't you shout to come and look, nor use 'em for your play.
Put the brishwood back again – and they'll be gone next day!

If you see the stable-door setting open wide;
If you see a tired horse lying down inside;
If your mother mends a coat cut about and tore;
If the lining's wet and warm – don't you ask no more!

If you meet King George's men, dressed in blue and red,
You be careful what you say, and mindful what is said.
If they call you 'pretty maid,' and chuck you 'neath the chin,
Don't you tell where no one is, nor yet where no one's been!

Knocks and footsteps round the house – whistles after dark –
You've no call for running out till the house-dogs bark.
Trusty's here, and *Pincher's* here, and see how dumb they lie –
They don't fret to follow when the Gentlemen go by!

If you do as you've been told, 'likely there's a chance,
You'll be give a dainty doll, all the way from France,
With a cap of Valenciennes, and a velvet hood —
A present from the Gentlemen, along o' being good!
   Five and twenty ponies,
   Trotting through the dark —
   Brandy for the Parson,
   'Baccy for the Clerk.
Them that asks no questions isn't told a lie —
Watch the wall, my darling, while the Gentlemen go by!

THE SLAVE'S DREAM

Beside the ungathered rice he lay,
His sickle in his hand;
His breast was bare, his matted hair
Was buried in the sand.
Again, in the mist and shadow of sleep,
He saw his Native Land.

Wide through the landscape of his dreams
The lordly Niger flowed;
Beneath the palm-trees on the plain
Once more a king he strode;
And heard the tinkling caravans
Descend the mountain-road.

He saw once more his dark-eyed queen
Among her children stand;
They clasped his neck, they kissed his cheeks,
They held him by the hand! –
A tear burst from the sleeper's lids
And fell into the sand.

And then at furious speed he rode
Along the Niger's bank;
His bridle-reins were golden chains,
And, with a martial clank,
At each leap he could feel his scabbard of steel
Smiting his stallion's flank.

Before him, like a blood-red flag,
The bright flamingoes flew;
From morn till night he followed their flight,
O'er plains where the tamarind grew,
Till he saw the roofs of Caffre huts,
And the ocean rose to view.

At night he heard the lion roar,
And the hyena scream,
And the river-horse, as he crushed the reeds
Beside some hidden stream;
And it passed, like a glorious roll of drums,
Through the triumph of his dream.

The forests, with their myriad tongues,
Shouted of liberty;
And the Blast of the Desert cried aloud,
With a voice so wild and free,
That he started in his sleep and smiled
At their tempestuous glee.

He did not feel the driver's whip
Nor the burning heat of day;
For Death had illumined the Land of Sleep,
And his lifeless body lay
A worn-out fetter, that the soul
Had broken and thrown away!

PERCY BYSSHE SHELLEY 1792–1822

LOVE'S PHILOSOPHY

The fountains mingle with the river
And the rivers with the ocean,
The winds of heaven mix for ever
With a sweet emotion;
Nothing in the world is single,
All things by a law divine
In one another's being mingle –
Why not I with thine?

See the mountains kiss high heaven
And the waves clasp one another;
No sister-flower would be forgiven
If it disdain'd its brother:

And the sunlight clasps the earth
And the moonbeams kiss the sea –
What are all these kissings worth,
If thou kiss not me?

A.E. HOUSMAN 1859–1936

LOVELIEST OF TREES, THE CHERRY NOW

Loveliest of trees, the cherry now
Is hung with bloom along the bough,
And stands about the woodland ride
Wearing white for Eastertide.

Now, of my threescore years and ten,
Twenty will not come again,
And take from seventy springs a score,
It only leaves me fifty more.

And since to look at things in bloom
Fifty springs are little room,
About the woodlands I will go
To see the cherry hung with snow.

LEIGH HUNT 1784–1859
ABOU BEN ADHEM

Abou Ben Adhem (may his tribe increase!)
Awoke one night from a deep dream of peace,
And saw, within the moonlight in his room,
Making it rich, and like a lily in bloom,
An angel writing in a book of gold: —
Exceeding peace had made Ben Adhem bold,
And to the presence in the room he said,
    'What writest thou?' — The vision raised its head,
And with a look made of all sweet accord,
Answered, 'The names of those who love the Lord.'
'And is mine one?' said Abou. 'Nay, not so,'
Replied the angel. Abou spoke more low,
But cheerly still, and said, 'I pray thee, then,
Write me as one that loves his fellow men.'
    The angel wrote, and vanished. The next night
It came again with a great wakening light,
And showed the names whom love of God had blest,
And lo! Ben Adhem's name led all the rest.

LEWIS CARROLL 1832–98

THE WALRUS AND THE CARPENTER

The sun was shining on the sea,
Shining with all his might;
He did his very best to make
The billows smooth and bright –
And this was odd, because it was
The middle of the night.

The moon was shining sulkily,
Because she thought the sun
Had got no business to be there
After the day was done –
'It's very rude of him,' she said,
'To come and spoil the fun!'

The sea was wet as wet could be,
The sands were dry as dry.
You could not see a cloud, because
No cloud was in the sky;
No birds were flying overhead –
There were no birds to fly.

The Walrus and the Carpenter
Were walking close at hand;
They wept like anything to see
Such quantities of sand –
'If this were only cleared away,'
They said, 'it would be grand!'

'If seven maids with seven mops
Swept it for half a year,
Do you suppose,' the Walrus said,
'That they could get it clear?'
'I doubt it,' said the Carpenter,
And shed a bitter tear.

'O Oysters, come and walk with us!'
The Walrus did beseech.
'A pleasant walk, a pleasant talk,
Along the briny beach;
We cannot do with more than four,
To give a hand to each.'

The eldest Oyster looked at him,
But never a word he said;
The eldest Oyster winked his eye,
And shook his heavy head –
Meaning to say he did not choose
To leave the oyster-bed.

But four young Oysters hurried up,
All eager for the treat;
Their coats were brushed, their faces washed,
Their shoes were clean and neat –
And this was odd, because, you know,
They hadn't any feet.

Four other Oysters followed them,
And yet another four;
And thick and fast they came at last,
And more, and more, and more –
All hopping through the frothy waves,
And scrambling to the shore.

The Walrus and the Carpenter
Walked on a mile or so,
And then they rested on a rock
Conveniently low –
And all the little Oysters stood
And waited in a row.

'The time has come,' the Walrus said,
'To talk of many things:
Of shoes — and ships — and sealing-wax —
Of cabbages — and kings —
And why the sea is boiling hot —
And whether pigs have wings.'

'But wait a bit,' the Oysters cried,
'Before we have our chat;
For some of us are out of breath,
And all of us are fat!'
'No hurry!' said the Carpenter.
They thanked him much for that.

'A loaf of bread,' the Walrus said,
'Is what we chiefly need;
Pepper and vinegar besides
Are very good indeed —
Now, if you're ready, Oysters dear,
We can begin to feed.'

'But not on us!' the Oysters cried,
Turning a little blue,
'After such kindness, that would be
A dismal thing to do!'
'The night is fine,' the Walrus said.
'Do you admire the view?'

'It was so kind of you to come!
And you are very nice!'
The Carpenter said nothing but,
'Cut us another slice.
I wish you were not quite so deaf —
I've had to ask you twice!'

'It seems a shame,' the Walrus said,
'To play them such a trick.
After we've brought them out so far,
And made them trot so quick!'
The Carpenter said nothing but,
'The butter's spread too thick!'

'I weep for you,' the Walrus said;
'I deeply sympathize.'
With sobs and tears he sorted out
Those of the largest size,
Holding his pocket-handkerchief
Before his streaming eyes.

'O Oysters,' said the Carpenter,
'You've had a pleasant run!
Shall we be trotting home again?'
But answer came there none —
And this was scarcely odd, because
They'd eaten every one.

DOVER BEACH

The sea is calm to-night.
The tide is full, the moon lies fair
Upon the straits; – on the French coast the light
Gleams and is gone; the cliffs of England stand,
Glimmering and vast, out in the tranquil bay.
Come to the window, sweet is the night-air!
Only, from the long line of spray
Where the sea meets the moon-blanch'd land,
Listen! you hear the grating roar
Of pebbles which the waves draw back, and fling,
At their return, up the high strand,
Begin, and cease, and then again begin,
With tremulous cadence slow, and bring
The eternal note of sadness in.

Sophocles long ago
Heard it on the Aegean, and it brought
Into his mind the turbid ebb and flow
Of human misery; we
Find also in the sound a thought,
Hearing it by this distant northern sea.

The Sea of Faith
Was once, too, at the full, and round earth's shore
Lay like the folds of a bright girdle furl'd.
But now I only hear
Its melancholy, long, withdrawing roar,
Retreating, to the breath
Of the night-wind, down the vast edges drear
And naked shingles of the world.

Ah, love, let us be true
To one another! for the world, which seems
To lie before us like a land of dreams,
So various, so beautiful, so new,
Hath really neither joy, nor love, nor light,
Nor certitude, nor peace, nor help for pain;
And we are here as on a darkling plain
Swept with confused alarms of struggle and flight,
Where ignorant armies clash by night.

JAMES K. BAXTER 1926-72

FARMHAND

You will see him light a cigarette
At the hall door careless, leaning his back
Against the wall, or telling some new joke
To a friend, or looking out into the secret night.

But always his eyes turn
To the dance floor and the girls drifting like flowers
Before the music that tears
Slowly in his mind an old wound open.

His red sunburnt face and hairy hands
Were not made for dancing or love-making
But rather the earth wave breaking
To the plough, and crops slow-growing as his mind.

He has no girl to run her fingers through
His sandy hair, and giggle at his side
When Sunday couples walk. Instead
He has his awkward hopes, his envious dreams to yarn to.

But ah in harvest watch him
Forking stooks, effortless and strong –
Or listening like a lover to the song
Clear, without fault, of a new tractor engine.

WILLIAM ERNEST HENLEY 1849–1903

INVICTUS

Out of the night that covers me,
  Black as the Pit from pole to pole,
I thank whatever gods may be
  For my unconquerable soul.

In the fell clutch of circumstance
  I have not winced nor cried aloud.
Under the bludgeonings of chance
  My head is bloody, but unbowed.

Beyond this place of wrath and tears
  Looms but the horror of the shade,
And yet the menace of the years
  Finds, and shall find, me unafraid.

It matters not how strait the gate,
  How charged with punishments the scroll,
I am the master of my fate:
  I am the captain of my soul.

JOHN GILLESPIE MAGEE 1922–41

HIGH FLIGHT (AN AIRMAN'S ECSTASY)

Oh, I have slipped the surly bonds of earth
And danced the skies on laughter-silvered wings;
Sunward I've climbed and joined the tumbling mirth
Of sun-split clouds – and done a hundred things
You have not dreamed of; wheeled and soared and swung
High in the sun-lit silence. Hovering there
I've chased the shouting wind along, and flung
My eager craft through footless halls of air;
Up, up the long, delirious, burning blue
I've topped the wind-swept heights with easy grace,
Where never lark nor even eagle flew;
And while, with silent lifting mind I've trod
The high untrespassed sanctity of space,
Put out my hand, and touched the face of God.

JAMES K. BAXTER 1926–72

HE WAIATA MO TE KARE

1

Up here at the wharepuni
That star at the kitchen window
Mentions your name to me.

Clear and bright like running water
It glitters above the rim of the range,
You in Wellington,
I at Jerusalem,

Woman, it is my wish
Our bodies should be buried in the same grave.

2

To others my love is a plaited kono
Full or empty,
With chunks of riwai,
Meat that stuck to the stones.

To you my love is a pendant
Of inanga greenstone,
Too hard to bite,
Cut from a boulder underground.

You can put it in a box
Or wear it over your heart.

One day it will grow warm,
One day it will tremble like a bed of rushes
And say to you with a man's tongue,
'Taku ngakau ki a koe!'

3

I have seen at evening
Two ducks fly down
To a pond together.

The whirring of their wings
Reminded me of you.

4

At the end of our lives
Te Atua will take pity
On the two whom he divided.

To the tribe he will give
Much talking, te pia and a loaded hangi.

To you and me he will give
A whare by the seashore
Where you can look for crabs and kina
And I can watch the waves
And from time to time see your face
With no sadness,
Te Kare o Nga Wai.

5

No rafter paintings,
No grass-stalk panels,
No Maori mass,

Christ and his Mother
Are lively Italians
Leaning forward to bless,

No taniko band on her head,
No feather cloak on his shoulder,

No stairway to heaven,
No tears of the albatross.

Here at Jerusalem
After ninety years
Of bungled opportunities,
I prefer not to invite you
Into the pakeha church.

6

Waves wash on the beaches.
They leave a mark for only a minute.
Each grey hair in my beard
Is there because of a sin,

The mirror shows me
An old tuatara,
He porangi, he tutua,
Standing in his dusty coat.

I do not think you wanted
Some other man.

I have walked barefoot from the tail of the fish to the nose
To say these words.

7

Hilltop behind hilltop,
A mile of green pungas
In the grey afternoon
Bow their heads to the slanting spears of rain.

In the middle room of the wharepuni
Kat is playing the guitar, –
'Let it be! Let it be!'

Don brings home a goat draped round his shoulders.
Tonight we'll eat roasted liver.

One day, it is possible,
Hoani and Hilary might join me here,
Tired of the merry-go-round.

E hine, the door is open,
There's a space beside me.

8

Those we knew when we were young,
None of them have stayed together,
All their marriages battered down like trees
By the winds of a terrible century.

I was a gloomy drunk.
You were a troubled woman.
Nobody would have given tuppence for our chances,
Yet our love did not turn to hate.

If you could fly this way, my bird,
One day before we both die,
I think you might find a branch to rest on.

I chose to live in a different way.

Today I cut the grass from the paths
With a new sickle,
Working till my hands were blistered.

I never wanted another wife.

9

Now I see you conquer age
As the prow of a canoe beats down
The plumes of Tangaroa.

You, straight-backed, a girl,
Your dark hair on your shoulders,
Lifting up our grandchild.

How you put them to shame,
All the flouncing girls!

Your face wears the marks of age
As a warrior his moko,
Double the beauty,
A soul like the great albatross

Who only nests in mid ocean
Under the eye of Te Ra.

You have broken the back of age.
I tremble to see it.

10

Taraiwa has sent us up a parcel of smoked eels
With skins like fine leather.
We steam them in the colander.
He tells us the heads are not for eating,

So I cut off two heads
And throw them out to Archibald,
The old tomcat. He growls as he eats
Simply because he's timid.

Earlier today I cut thistles
Under the trees in the graveyard,
And washed my hands afterwards,
Sprinkling the sickle with water.

That's the life I lead,
Simple as a stone,
And all that makes it less than good, Te Kare,
Is that you are not beside me.

W.H. AUDEN 1907–73

NIGHT MAIL
Commentary for a G.PO. Film

I

This is the Night Mail crossing the Border,
Bringing the cheque and the postal order,

Letters for the rich, letters for the poor,
The shop at the corner, the girl next door.

Pulling up Beattock, a steady climb:
The gradient's against her, but she's on time.

Past cotton-grass and moorland boulder
Shovelling white steam over her shoulder,

Snorting noisily as she passes
Silent miles of wind-bent grasses.

Birds turn their heads as she approaches,
Stare from bushes at her blank-faced coaches.

Sheep-dogs cannot turn her course;
They slumber on with paws across.

In the farm she passes no one wakes,
But a jug in a bedroom gently shakes.

II

Dawn freshens, her climb is done.
Down towards Glasgow she descends,
Towards the steam tugs yelping down a glade of cranes
Towards the fields of apparatus, the furnaces
Set on the dark plain like gigantic chessmen.
All Scotland waits for her:
In dark glens, beside pale-green lochs
Men long for news.

III

Letters of thanks, letters from banks,
Letters of joy from girl and boy,
Receipted bills and invitations
To inspect new stock or to visit relations,
And applications for situations,
And timid lovers' declarations,
And gossip, gossip from all the nations,
News circumstantial, news financial,
Letters with holiday snaps to enlarge in,
Letters with faces scrawled on the margin,
Letters from uncles, cousins, and aunts,
Letters to Scotland from the South of France,
Letters of condolence to Highlands and Lowlands
Written on paper of every hue,
The pink, the violet, the white and the blue,
The chatty, the catty, the boring, the adoring,
The cold and official and the heart's outpouring,
Clever, stupid, short and long,
The typed and the printed and the spelt all wrong.

IV

Thousands are still asleep,
Dreaming of terrifying monsters
Or of friendly tea beside the band in Cranston's or Crawford's:
Asleep in working Glasgow, asleep in well-set Edinburgh,
Asleep in granite Aberdeen,
They continue their dreams,
But shall wake soon and hope for letters,
And none will hear the postman's knock
Without a quickening of the heart,
For who can bear to feel himself forgotten?

ROBERT FROST 1874–1963

NOTHING GOLD CAN STAY

Nature's first green is gold,
Her hardest hue to hold.
Her early leaf's a flower;
But only so an hour.
Then leaf subsides to leaf,
So Eden sank to grief,
So dawn goes down to day
Nothing gold can stay.

FORGETFULNESS

The name of the author is the first to go
followed obediently by the title, the plot,
the heartbreaking conclusion, the entire novel
which suddenly becomes one you have never read, never
   even heard of.

It is as if, one by one, the memories you used to harbor
decided to retire to the southern hemisphere of the brain,
to a little fishing village where there are no phones.

Long ago you kissed the names of the nine Muses goodbye
and watched the quadratic equation pack its bag,
and even now as you memorize the order of the planets,

something else is slipping away, a state flower perhaps,
the address of an uncle, the capital of Paraguay.

Whatever it is you are struggling to remember
it is not poised on the tip of your tongue,
not even lurking in some obscure corner of your spleen.

It has floated away down a dark mythological river
whose name begins with an *L* as far as you can recall,
well on your own way to oblivion where you will join those
who have even forgotten how to swim and how to ride a bicycle.

No wonder you rise in the middle of the night
to look up the date of a famous battle in a book on war.
No wonder the moon in the window seems to have drifted
out of a love poem that you used to know by heart.

A.A. MILNE 1882–1956

DISOBEDIENCE

James James
Morrison Morrison
Weatherby George Dupree
Took great
Care of his Mother
Though he was only three.
James James Said to his Mother,
'Mother,' he said, said he;
'You must never go down to the end of the town,
  if you don't go down with me.'

James James
Morrison's Mother
Put on a golden gown.
James James Morrison's Mother
Drove to the end of the town.
James James Morrison's Mother
Said to herself, said she:
'I can get right down to the end of the town and
  be back in time for tea.'

King John
Put up a notice,
'LOST or STOLEN or STRAYED!
JAMES JAMES
MORRISON'S MOTHER
SEEMS TO HAVE BEEN MISLAID.
LAST SEEN
WANDERING VAGUELY:
QUITE OF HER OWN ACCORD,
SHE TRIED TO GET DOWN TO THE END OF THE
TOWN – FORTY SHILLINGS REWARD!'

James James
Morrison Morrison
(Commonly known as Jim)
Told his
Other relations
Not to go blaming *him*.
James James
Said to his Mother,
'Mother,' he said, said he,
'You must *never* go down to the end of the town
without consulting me.'

James James
Morrison's Mother
Hasn't been heard of since.
King John
Said he was sorry,
So did the Queen and Prince.
King John
(Somebody told me)
Said to a man he knew:
'If people go down to the end of the town, well,
what can *anyone* do?'

(*Now then, very softly*)
J. J.
M. M.
W. G. du P.
Took great
C/O his M*****
Though he was only 3.
J. J.
Said to his M*****
'M*****,' he said, said he:
'You-must-never-go-down-to-the-end-of-the-town-
if-you-don't-go-down-with ME!'

LAURIS EDMOND 1924–2000

LATE SONG

It's a still morning, quiet and cloudy
the kind of grey day I like best;
they'll be here soon, the little kids first,
creeping up to try and frighten me,
then the tall young men, the slim boy
with the marvellous smile, the dark girl
subtle and secret; and the others,
the parents, my children, my friends –

and I think: these truly are my weather
my grey mornings and my rain at night,
my sparkling afternoons and my birdcall at daylight;
they are my game of hide and seek, my song
that flies from a high window. They are
my dragonflies dancing on silver water.

Without them I cannot move forward, I am
a broken signpost, a train fetched up on
a small siding, a dry voice buzzing in the ears;
for they are also my blunders
and my forgiveness for blundering,
my road to the stars and my seagrass chair
in the sun. They fly where I cannot follow

and I – I am their branch, their tree.
My song is of the generations, it echoes
the old dialogue of the years; it is the tribal
chorus that no one may sing alone.

RUTH DALLAS 1919–

DEEP IN THE HILLS

Once I thought the land I had loved and known
Lay curled in my inmost self; musing alone
In the quiet room I unfolded the folded sea,
Unlocked the forest and the lonely tree,
Hill and mountain valley beach and stone,
All these, I said, are here and exist in me.

But now I know it is I who exist in the land;
My inmost self is blown like a grain of sand
Along the windy beach, and is only free
To wander among the mountains, enter the tree,
To turn again a sea-worn stone in the hand,
Because these things exist outside of me.

O far from the quiet room my spirit fills
The familiar valleys, is folded deep in the hills.

GLENN COLQUHOUN 1964–

MOTHERS, LOVE YOUR SONS

Mothers, love your sons.
Love your big, dumb sons,
Your idiot sons,
Your swaggering sons,
Your awkward sons,
Your irresponsible sons and their indestructible limbs.

Love their red and bleeding knees.
Love their clear, uncluttered eyes.
Love their stumbling, foal-like hands.
Love their necks just asking to be wrung.

Love their shoes lost in the neighbour's yard.
Love their badly ironed clothes.
Love their terrible haircuts.
Love their empty tanks of petrol.

Love their awkwardness at airports leaving
for a world they were expecting to change.

Love their awkwardness at airports returning
from a world they were expecting to change.

Love the hair on their chins like
a small lawn of badly cut grass.

Love their broken-hearted girlfriends
calling in the middle of the night.

Love your northern sons,
Your southern sons,
Your eastern sons,
Your western sons.

Love your granite sons,
Your iron sons,
Your crystal sons,
Your paper sons.

Love your rising sons,
Your blazing sons,
Your noonday sons,
Your setting sons.

Mothers, love your sons.
Love your big, dumb sons,
Your idiot sons,
Your swaggering sons,
Your awkward sons,
Your irresponsible sons and their indestructible limbs.

Because they die so fast,

So awkwardly, lankily, idiotically, swaggeringly fast,
With everybody staring at them,
On a Friday night, with a wicked grin,
In the moment of their greatest triumph,

When they will always be the last to know,

The last, that is, except for you.

SAM HUNT 1946–

FOUR BOW-WOW POEMS

I

You woke my mother up this morning
At six o'clock with your barking

So she took away your barks
And put them in the bow-wow box

She tied you up she took your barks away
Now all you do is smile at strangers all day

You aren't a guard dog anymore
You aren't even a dog anymore!

2

I don't really think I like
A dog that can't bark when he likes

So all by myself this afternoon
I took the bow-wow box down

It was hidden in behind a lot of books
And I gave you back eleven big barks

You've run outside to use them up
I think you've woken the baby up!

3
Look, here are some simple facts:
You'll find in the poetry books
One thousand and twelve poems about cats

There are all sorts of poems about cats:
Cats chasing rats and cats wearing hats
And cats that simply sit on mats

But you look for bow-wow poetry
And it's quite a different story
Right now there are only three

And one more makes four . . .

They often ask me why
I write this bow-wow poetry

I'll tell you
And cross-my-heart it's true

I've got nothing else to do

THOMAS BRACKEN 1843–98

NOT UNDERSTOOD

Not understood, we move along asunder;
Our paths grow wider as the seasons creep
Along the years; we marvel and we wonder
Why life is life, and then we fall asleep
    Not understood.

Not understood, we gather false impressions
And hug them closer as the years go by;
Till virtues often seem to us transgressions;
And thus men rise and fall, and live and die
    Not understood.

Not understood! Poor souls with stunted vision
Oft measure giants with their narrow gauge;
The poisoned shafts of falsehood and derision
Are oft impelled 'gainst those who mould the age,
    Not understood.

Not understood! The secret springs of action
Which lie beneath the surface and the show,
Are disregarded; with self-satisfaction
We judge our neighbours, and they often go
    Not understood.

Not understood! How trifles often change us!
The thoughtless sentence and the fancied slight
Destroy long years of friendship, and estrange us,
And on our souls there falls a freezing blight;
    Not understood.

Not understood! How many breasts are aching
For lack of sympathy! Ah! day by day
How many cheerless, lonely hearts are breaking!
How many noble spirits pass away,
    Not understood.

O God! that men would see a little clearer,
Or judge less harshly where they cannot see!
O God! that men would draw a little nearer
To one another, – they'd be nearer Thee,
    And understood.

ROGER MCGOUGH 1937–

AT LUNCHTIME

When the bus stopped suddenly
to avoid damaging
a mother and child in the road,
the younglady in the green hat sitting opposite,
was thrown across me,
and not being one to miss an opportunity
I started to make love.

At first, she resisted,
saying that it was too early in the morning,
and too soon after breakfast,
and anyway, she found me repulsive.
But when I explained
that this being a nuclearage
the world was going to end at lunchtime,
she took off her green hat,
put her busticket into her pocket
and joined in the exercise.

The buspeople,
and there were many of them,
were shockedandsurprised,
and amusedandannoyed.
But when the word got around
that the world was going to end at lunchtime,
they put their pride in their pockets
with their bustickets
and made love one with the other.
And even the busconductor,
feeling left out,
climbed into the cab,
and struck up some sort of relationship with the driver.

That night,
on the bus coming home,
we were all a little embarrassed.
Especially me and the younglady in the green hat.
And we all started to say
in different ways
how hasty and foolish we had been.
But then, always having been a bitofalad,
I stood up and said it was a pity
that the world didnt nearly end every lunchtime,
and that we could always pretend.
And then it happened...

Quick asa crash
we all changed partners,
and soon the bus was aquiver
with white, mothball bodies doing naughty things.

And the next day
and everyday
In everybus
In everystreet
In everytown
In everycountry

People pretended
that the world was coming to an end at lunchtime.
It still hasn't.
Although in a way it has.

ACKNOWLEDGEMENTS

The publishers would like to acknowledge the following for permission to reproduce copyright material.

'The Beach' by Liam McKinstry. Reprinted by permission of Liam McKinstry, Kathleen Hickey, and Donald McKinstry.

'Rain' and 'No Ordinary Sun' by Hone Tuwhare. Reprinted by permission of Hone Tuwhare.

'Arawata Bill' and 'The Magpies' by Denis Glover. Reprinted by permission of Pia Glover and the Denis Glover Literary Estate.

'The Highwayman' by Alfred Noyes reprinted by permission of The Society of Authors as the Literary Representative of the estate of Alfred Noyes.

'A Drowning' by Charlotte Trevella. Reprinted by permission of Charlotte and Geraldine Trevella.

'The Road Not Taken', 'Nothing Gold Can Stay' and 'Stopping by Woods on a Snowy Evening' from *The Poetry of Robert Frost* edited by Edward Connery Lathem, published by Jonathan Cape. Reprinted by permission of The Random House Group Ltd.

'Counting the Cent' by Trudi Sutcliffe. Reprinted by permission of Trudi Sutcliffe.

'High Country Weather', 'Poem in the Matukituki Valley', 'The Maori Jesus', 'Ballad of Calvary Street' and 'Farmhand' by James K. Baxter. Reprinted by permission of Dr Paul Miller, Literary Advisor to the James K. Baxter Trust.

Reprinted by permission of Sam Hunt.

'At Lunchtime' by Roger McGough (© Roger McGough 1967) from *The Mersey Sound* is reproduced by permission of PFD (www.pfd.co.uk) on behalf of Roger McGough.

Craig Potton Publishing has made every effort to trace the copyright holders of all material contained in this book and attribute the correct acknowledgements. If any omissions have occurred, we would appreciate being contacted directly to rectify the mistake.

INDEX OF POETS

INDEX OF FIRST LINES

A

B

D

E

G

H

I

J

L

M

N

U

W

Y